THE
HUSTLE
MINDSET

How to build a successful start-up
through grit and grind

REECE BORG

Rethink

First published in Great Britain in 2026
by Rethink Press (www.rethinkpress.com)

© Copyright Reece Borg

All rights reserved. No part of this publication may be reproduced, stored in or introduced into a retrieval system, or transmitted, in any form, or by any means (electronic, mechanical, photocopying, recording or otherwise) without the prior written permission of the publisher.

The right of Reece Borg to be identified as the author of this work has been asserted by him in accordance with the Copyright, Designs and Patents Act 1988.

This book is sold subject to the condition that it shall not, by way of trade or otherwise, be lent, resold, hired out, or otherwise circulated without the publisher's prior consent in any form of binding or cover other than that in which it is published and without a similar condition including this condition being imposed on the subsequent purchaser.

Cover image © Shutterstock | Wirestock Creators

Contents

Introduction	1
1 What Separates Hustlers From Dreamers	7
Resilience	9
Embrace risk	12
Be proactive	14
Adapt	16
Don't procrastinate	19
Be persistent	21
Be decisive	23
Self-confidence	26
2 Finding An Idea That Works	29
A different path	30
Where the ideas come from	33
The power of trends	37
Busting the 'passion' myth	39
Don't overthink it	40
3 A Reality Check: Validating Your Idea	45
Good idea, bad business	46
Viability	48
Market research	50

4 **No Excuses, Just Action: How To Stop Overthinking And Start Doing** 63
   Momentum 64
   Business plan 66
   Build the foundations 68
   Prioritising 71
   Fear and uncertainty 74

5 **Testing Ideas At Lightning Speed – The Value Of An MVP** 79
   Early validation 82
   Alternative MVPs 84
   Digital MVPs 85
   Using tech to build and validate your MVP 87
   Finding testers and collecting feedback 92
   Negative feedback 96

6 **Partnerships** 99
   Qualities to look for 101
   Setting expectations 106
   Due diligence 112
   Contracts 113
   When things go wrong 116

7 **Building A Team Of Believers** 119
   Recruitment 120
   An over-the-top hiring process 122
   The interview process 126
   Qualities to prioritise 128
   A two-way street 133
   Employment contracts 134

8	**A 360-Degree Team**	**137**
	The 360-degree philosophy	138
	How to build a 360-degree team	142
	Disruptors	147
	Trust, celebration and shared wins	149
9	**The Quiet Power Of Solid Systems And Processes**	**153**
	Get your house in order	154
	Managing the money	157
	Managing the backend	162
	Cyber security	169
10	**Time Waits For No One**	**175**
	'Busy' doesn't mean 'successful'	179
	Don't let yourself drift	180
	How to best use your time and resources	182
	The benefit of hindsight	192
11	**Coping Under Pressure**	**195**
	Embrace the mess	196
	Dealing with the pressure and uncertainty	198
	Mental resilience	200
	Control your physical state	203
	Don't self-sabotage	206
	Failure is a mindset	210
12	**When People Try To Hustle Your Hustle**	**213**
	Beware cling-ons	214
	Spotting the red flags	217
	The cost of keeping the peace	220
	How to protect your hustle	222

13 Investing In Other Businesses   **225**
    Shared success   226
    Finding good investments   228
    Good business or great business?   232
    Investment due diligence   234

14 The Exit   **241**
    Thinking long-term   242
    Always be exit-ready   245
    When's the right time to exit?   247
    Maximising the sale price   250
    The key financial metrics   252
    Managing the sale   253
    Misconceptions about selling   255
    No deal   258
    Life after the sale   259

Conclusion   **261**

Acknowledgements   **267**

The Author   **269**

Introduction

School and I were never a good match. I spoke my mind, and teachers didn't like that. Most of my time was spent in the Learning Support Unit, not because I struggled with the work, but because I refused to just sit down and stay quiet. By the time I left at 16, I had only one GCSE (in art) to my name. To top it off, at our end-of-year assembly, the teachers thought it would be funny to vote me 'most likely to end up in jail'. Thanks for the vote of confidence.

The thing is, I love learning – I just had to find the right environment. Out here, in the real world, every day is a lesson. If you're paying attention, life will teach you everything you need to know. That would've sounded like a nightmare to my 16-year-old self, but the truth is, it's the only way to win.

School doesn't prepare you for real life. It churns out employees, not entrepreneurs. It drills in the same outdated syllabus that's been collecting dust for generations but skips the stuff that actually matters, like how to make money, take risks and, yes, how to survive. The UK is full of entrepreneurs, but that's no thanks to our education system. We succeed in spite of it.

Since leaving school with that less than ringing endorsement, I've never looked back. I've founded and built more than two dozen companies. Some of my start-ups fizzled and died, for various reasons; others made a lot of money. My life has been one constant hustle, which is where the Hustle Mindset name came from, and I have learned loads about what works along the way. Unlike my old school, I've been more than willing to share the secrets to the Hustle Mindset with anyone and everyone, no matter their background. To my mind, the more entrepreneurs we have, the better for everyone.

I've spent years supporting SMEs, real businesses run by real people trying to make things happen. Some needed help scaling, while others needed a shove in the right direction to get their start-up off the ground. Many just needed to hear the truth about what it actually takes to succeed. I never promise anyone overnight success, but I can show them what works, what doesn't and how to keep moving forward even when everything is stacked against you.

I was getting asked for advice so often that I started another business, RB Business Consultancy, as

INTRODUCTION

a vehicle for working with founders on real decisions in real businesses. When that took off, it made sense to get it all down in a book. That's what you are reading now. It contains everything I have learned about how to build a successful start-up, through grit and grind.

This won't be for everyone. I know that. There are two kinds of entrepreneurs. There are the ones who want a business that ticks along, covers the bills and keeps life predictable. There's nothing wrong with that. If your goal is a steady income, a manageable workload and the freedom to live on your own terms, that's a win. For some people, that is success. But there's another kind of entrepreneur, and if you're holding this book, the chances are you're one of them. You're the type who's all in, not just building a business to survive and have a decent life, but building a future to grow into. For you, success isn't a number in the bank, a round of applause or a one-time milestone. It's a mindset. A way of thinking. A way of moving through the world. When you think about the business you want to create, you want it to be the best, to push limits and make an impact. You'll be the type to spot opportunities others miss and take calculated risks when the average person would rather stay comfortable. You'll never be happy to just stand still.

This book is for those entrepreneurs – the ones who don't clock out and who see business as a tool not just for income, but for impact. The real hustle is growth – personal, professional and financial.

I won't sugarcoat the Hustle Mindset: everything I've learned, I learned the hard way. I've built businesses and lost them. I've made mistakes that cost me time, money and sleep. But those failures taught me as much, if not more, than my wins. Now, I'm sharing those lessons with you.

I didn't write this book to stroke my ego, or to give you some recycled business-school nonsense. I want to tell you how it really is. There's no fluff, no theory, just practical, straight-talking advice from someone who has been in the trenches, taken the punches and figured out what works. If you're looking for a neat little roadmap with guaranteed success, you're in the wrong place. If, however, you want raw, unfiltered insights from someone who has been through it all and come out the other side, you'll find a lot of value here.

A lot of what you'll read here isn't conventional. It won't be the stuff you hear in polished TED Talks or from start-up gurus preaching hustle culture from the comfort of their corporate-backed safety net. This is real talk, based on real experience. Some of it you might agree with, some of it you won't, but every lesson in here has been battle-tested in the real world.

No entrepreneur is born with the hustle mindset. We are all sharpened by grit and grind. In the beginning, we make decisions on gut feeling. We're chasing every shiny opportunity, saying yes to too much, thinking we can do it all. We're running on caffeine, adrenaline and a half-broken laptop.

Then the realisation hits: this doesn't scale. This won't last.

INTRODUCTION

So, we adapt. We start seeing what works and what burns us. We start recognising patterns. Our gut gets smarter. Our thinking gets sharper.

Success won't come because you read some leadership blog. Nor will this book do the work for you. No book can. What it will do, though, is show you how to survive, adapt and build something that lasts, no matter how many times you get knocked down. Then it is over to you. You'll still get screwed over, lose money, maybe miss payroll or back the wrong person, but if you don't fold, you *will* build something truly great.

You don't need to be the loudest in the room, or even the smartest, but if you're willing to think differently, stay sharp and do the work then this book is for you.

Let's get into it.

1
What Separates Hustlers From Dreamers

Being labelled 'most likely to end up in jail' by your teachers is never a good start to adult life. But there's a twist to this story: I wasn't alone. I had a partner in misfortune, my mate Sam (not his real name). Sam in fact did live up to the label given to us by those teachers before we left school, ending up behind bars.

Sam and I shared the same rebellious spirit and a passionate drive to defy a system that we knew never had our best interests at heart. But one careless decision set our paths on different tracks.

While in Thailand on holiday, Sam made a choice that changed everything. When out for a drink, he casually asked for more ice. In that part of the world, 'ice' is street slang for crystal meth. The bartender misinterpreted his order and, by the time Sam understood what was happening, he had been handed some 'ice' and, out of curiosity, tried it. He liked it so much that he carried on doing it when he was back in the UK. A few years later, Sam was a shell of the man he once was: distrustful, embittered and lost in a haze where reality and illusion blurred. He was sectioned multiple times over the years.

I share this story because that choice could have been anyone's. We're all just one impulsive decision away from derailing our lives. But the reverse is also true: one wise decision, one significant step, one moment of clarity, can change everything. I always say we live two lives: the second begins when you finally realise you only have one shot.

It's far too easy to settle for 'good enough'. Most people will achieve a bit of success in their careers and be satisfied. A few – very few – may be bold enough to go it alone, but, after trying something and failing, they retreat to the safety of a day job. Fewer still will start a business and manage to make it a real success, sticking with it through thick and thin. That's the difference between dreamers and hustlers. Dreamers have ambition, but they back off when challenges arise. Hustlers press on, taking action, making mistakes, learning quickly and relentlessly pushing forward.

What are you? A dreamer, or a hustler? The fact that you've picked up this book indicates that you might be a hustler. Or, are at least dreaming of being a hustler. Maybe, though, you are worried about whether you've got what it takes? You may not have been labelled 'most likely to end up in jail', but there could still be a part of you that has listened to the doomsayers who tell you to play it safe. (The majority of people are like this, even those closest to you.)

To get started, let's see what you are made of. The following eight sections detail the qualities you need to be a hustler. As you are reading them, think about yourself. Does this describe you? Don't worry if not all of them do. But don't judge yourself too harshly – I'll bet that you probably have demonstrated some of these qualities, but you perhaps haven't given yourself credit for it. I think you'll surprise yourself. If not, don't worry – you'll learn the hard way. Only kidding. Well, sort of.

OK, let's look at what it takes to be a true hustler.

Resilience

Resilience is about keeping going, no matter what. To date, I've had a go at twenty-four companies. Some have failed; some never got that far. Some I've sold, and some I'm still running now. It's never been about getting everything right the first time; it's about pushing through, learning and adapting. You can make a hundred mistakes, but if you get it right once, that one success can change everything. The key is to keep moving forward, no matter what setbacks come your way. That's resilience – just *refusing* to quit.

Let me share a story about one of my ventures that didn't end well. It wasn't through lack of trying.

I was running a successful training company called Trusted Training 4U. It was thriving, but growth requires taking risks. I learned about something called 'end point assessments', an external validation for apprenticeships that seemed to have strong potential. I decided to set up a new company to do this, calling it the Education and Care Qualification Network (ECQN), but before we could offer the service, we needed to secure accreditation from the awarding body OFQUAL, which was quite daunting. Oh, and I knew nothing about end point assessments. I was, however, determined.

At around the same time I was doing this, I had also recently taken on a restaurant lease and begun a full refurb project, and I was still running Trusted Training 4U. With that in mind, I thought it best to bring in an expert to handle the OFQUAL application and hired a supposedly experienced internal quality assessor. Unfortunately, my trust in the individual who I brought in to help me grow the company in a new niche was ultimately misplaced. A lot of troubling issues quickly came to light that created a period of stress, confusion, uncertainty and loss of control. After a short time, it became clear that we couldn't work together. But when this person offered to buy me out for a significant sum, many advised against taking the money, and something felt off. Eventually, the tables turned and I bought him out instead. It was a draining process, both emotionally and financially.

Then, just as I regained control, the COVID-19 pandemic struck, completely disrupting the market. Overnight, the assessment business became a liability.

Colleges abruptly closed, apprenticeship programmes stopped and I was left with mounting debts. I exhausted every option to keep the business afloat – personal loans, government bounce-back loans – but eventually, the debts overwhelmed me.

Despite my best efforts to sell the business, the only potential deal on the table collapsed unexpectedly. With no alternative left, I had to liquidate. It was a bitter pill to swallow. Yet, in this dark time, I realised that my strength wasn't measured in success alone, but in the resilience needed to keep moving forward and fighting back, regardless of setbacks. That is what kept me going then, and it has been an invaluable quality in my other businesses since.

REFLECTION EXERCISE

Think about your own life and career to date. In a journal or notebook, write down examples of when you have:

- **Adapted quickly to challenges:** Resilience is adapting swiftly when faced with setbacks. Each challenge presents an opportunity to learn and pivot.
- **Trusted your instincts:** Even when the advice pointed in another direction, you have listened closely to your intuition.
- **Kept going despite failures:** Real entrepreneurship isn't defined by uninterrupted success but by the courage and determination to persist through failure.

THE HUSTLE MINDSET

Embrace risk

Risk isn't just part of the game – it *is* the game. Every move, every decision, every investment carries weight and, for me, it's never been about playing it safe. It's been about backing myself, time and time again, even when it meant putting everything on the line.

I've never shied away from saying that I've had a go at a fair few companies, and not all of them have come good. But one thing that's been consistent through all of those efforts is that I've always gone all in. No half-measures. No safety nets. Just the belief that if I pushed hard enough, if I worked smart enough, I could make it happen.

There were times when I put every penny I had into a business, leaving myself with absolutely nothing, betting it all so that it *had* to work. I took out loans, personally guaranteed them, knowing full well that if it didn't pan out, I'd be the one picking up the pieces. And yeah, I lost. More than once. Three times, to be exact. Three times I lost everything and had to start over from scratch. With no money, no backup plan, just sheer determination and a refusal to stay down.

Most people would have quit after the first time; certainly after the second. But that's the difference between those who dream about success and those who build it. Every failure is just a step closer to figuring it out, another lesson learned, another piece of the puzzle. Eventually, the effort, the risks and the setbacks start to pay off, because the people who make it aren't the ones who never fall, they're the ones who refuse to stay down. Everyone who is successful will have failed at some point.

I've always found that failure makes me want to do more. I double down. To finish the story about the end point assessments where I ended up in debt and had to liquidate the company, I didn't give it all up, however bleak it looked. And it did look pretty bleak for a time, not least because I had to move back in with my mum and dad and sell an investment property. That was horrible. It wasn't like I didn't enjoy being with them, but once you've moved on, you've moved on. I knew I would be better off on my own.

After paying back my debts, I had £16k left over from the property sale. I picked myself up and started another business, this time in the financial services sector. To show how serious I was, I spent a lot of that £16k on upfront payment of six months' rental on a flat. I needed space to myself and a clear head. This deposit was a stake in the ground. It put me back on my feet and meant that I had to stay on my feet or I would be back with my mum and dad in half a year. I had to believe in myself and take that risk. It paid off. Things got a bit squeaky for a while and I got down to my last few pounds, but then I was on the up-and-up. Ultimately, I created a really successful business.

In the end, the biggest risk isn't losing money or starting over. It's never trying at all.

REFLECTION EXERCISE

Think about your own life and career to date. Note down examples of when you have:

- **Committed fully to a vision:** Success doesn't come from half-measures. Fully investing your resources, time and energy into your ideas significantly increases your chance of success.
- **Invested in yourself:** Even in the toughest circumstances, backing yourself – through investments, commitments, or personal guarantees – reinforces your drive to succeed.
- **Turned a setback into motivation:** Failure is fuel – setbacks can ignite determination and inspire even greater effort.

Be proactive

One of the most important lessons I've learned about business is that nothing just happens – you have to *make* it happen. That's the difference between people who succeed and people who don't. Some people sit around waiting for the perfect opportunity, the right moment or for things to just fall into place. Others get up, go out and create those opportunities for themselves. That's proactivity. That's the mindset that separates those who win from those who watch.

Being proactive means always pushing forward, always looking for the next move and never sitting still, just hoping things will sort themselves out. It means taking control of your business, of your future and of every situation you find yourself in. When you're proactive, you're not reacting to life – you're dictating it. You're setting the pace. You're making decisions before problems arise and putting yourself in the best position to succeed.

What about people who aren't proactive? They wait. They make excuses. They blame their circumstances, the market, the timing – everything but themselves. They tell themselves they'll start when they have more money, more knowledge, more connections. And before they know it, years have passed and they're still in the same place, wondering why nothing's changed.

I know a guy who is always talking about how he is going to start a business. Every time I see him, he has a new idea. One week it's e-commerce, the next it's property, then it's stocks. But every time, it's just talk. He'll research for months, watch YouTube videos and make plans, but he never actually starts anything. He wants the success, but he isn't willing to take the risks, put in the work and push through the challenges. That kind of ambition without action gets you nowhere.

When you're proactive, you don't wait for things to be perfect – you just start. You act. You test ideas. You make moves even when you don't have all the answers. You don't wait for doors to open; you kick them down. Being proactive means that while everyone else is standing still, you're already ten steps ahead, making things happen.

At the end of the day, success isn't about luck, timing or talent. It's about movement. If you're always pushing forward, always doing, always making moves, you're already ahead of 99% of people. Hustlers don't wait. They don't hesitate. They are proactive, take control and make things happen.

REFLECTION EXERCISE

Think about your own life and career to date. Note down examples of when you have:

- **Chosen action over perfection:** Waiting for perfect conditions is a mistake. Real progress comes from taking action despite uncertainty or imperfection.
- **Taken control over your destiny:** Proactive people shape their circumstances, rather than being shaped by them. They dictate outcomes, rather than react passively.
- **Learned by doing:** Testing ideas, learning from the outcomes and iterating quickly are key to entrepreneurial success.

Adapt

If there's one thing that's kept me in the game, it's my adaptability. I've started businesses in everything – from a dog swimming pool company, to a restaurant, to a training company, to a fintech app, to a business energy claims firm. Completely different industries, requiring completely different skill sets. But the one thing that is essential to all of them? The ability to adapt. If you can't adapt, you're done. It's as simple as that.

Business isn't static. The world isn't static. Things are constantly moving, changing, evolving and being updated and if you're not moving with them, you're falling behind. Take now, for example. We're in the middle of a digital revolution and if you're still running your business the way you were five or ten years ago, you're already behind the curve. You have to be able to change with the times. You need to be ahead of the shift, not trying to catch up once it's happened.

The people who win in business aren't the ones who stick to what's comfortable. They're the ones who see what's coming, pivot when they need to and don't get stuck in the past. The ones who refuse to adapt? They get left behind, wondering why nothing's working anymore.

This is another lesson I learned the hard way, in one of my earliest business ventures. Aged eighteen, I spotted a good market for bongs and decided to act, launching a company called Urban Paradise. I bought bongs in bulk from a wholesaler and flipped them on eBay. It wasn't flashy, but it was smart business. Before long, I was pulling in £2,000 to £3,000 a month, a solid haul for a teenager. I was buying them in at between £6 and £10 and selling for £25 to £45, so not bad profit margins either. Then, in one swift move, eBay shut it all down by banning the sale of drug paraphernalia. Just like that, my business vanished overnight.

That experience hit me hard. It showed me that a whole business can disappear in a single click, through no fault of your own. It drove home the point that if you're serious about building something, you must always have a Plan B, preferably a Plan B, C, D and E. A little tip here: always try to save enough money so that, if something does go wrong, you can fund yourself while you pivot. Even when you've got a good thing going, always have it in the back of your mind that it can end at any time.

That experience was my first real lesson in what it takes to be an entrepreneur: taking action, learning from every setback, adapting and relentlessly pushing forward, even when the game changes in an instant.

You don't need to be an expert in everything, but you do need to be willing to learn, evolve and change direction when the world demands it. The market doesn't care about what worked yesterday; it only cares about what works now.

Hustlers stay sharp, stay flexible and stay ahead, because in business, it's not the strongest or the smartest that survive, it's the ones who adapt.

REFLECTION EXERCISE

Think about your own life and career to date. Note down examples of when you have:

- **Diversified your plans:** Relying on a single approach or revenue stream is risky because circumstances can quickly change, leaving you vulnerable.

- **Prepared for sudden changes:** External factors outside your control, like regulatory changes or market disruptions, can come into effect instantly. Preparation and resilience are key.
- **Made an effort to keep learning and evolving:** Continuous learning and a willingness to pivot your business strategies help to maintain relevance in a fast-changing world.

Don't procrastinate

Acting with urgency has been a game-changer in my business journey. Too often, I've seen individuals with brilliant ideas stall, not because they lacked potential, but because they hesitated, overthought, let opportunities slip through their fingers or just faffed around with things that aren't important. Procrastination is the silent killer of progress.

Consider this: studies indicate that 20–25% of people are chronic procrastinators.[1] That's a significant portion of the population who are consistently delaying actions that could propel them forwards. In the workplace, the numbers are even more alarming.

---

1   DJ Ferrari, 'The prevalence of procrastination', *Psychology Today* (16 October 2020), www.psychologytoday.com/us/blog/still-procrastinating/202010/the-prevalence-procrastination, accessed December 2025

A staggering 88% of workers surveyed admit to procrastinating for at least an hour a day on the job.[2]

Think about the edge you can gain by simply having a bit of urgency. While others are stalling, caught up in indecision or distraction, you're making moves, seizing opportunities and setting the pace. Acting with urgency doesn't mean rushing blindly ahead; it means recognising the value of time and making deliberate, swift decisions to capitalise on the moment.

Procrastination doesn't just delay the completion of tasks; it has tangible consequences. In a dynamic market, delays can result in missed opportunities. Rest assured, while you are 'waiting for the right time', a competitor will be swooping in to make money out of the same idea. If it's a good one, someone else will have it too.

Here's the kicker, though: while many acknowledge the pitfalls of procrastination, few take steps to combat it. It's not just about managing time, it's about managing emotions, overcoming the fear of failure and breaking the cycle of inaction. Urgency is about both valuing your own time and understanding that every moment wasted comes with an opportunity cost. Hustlers push past the comfort of delay and embrace the momentum of immediate action. While

---

2   D Foroux, 'Procrastination Study: 88% of the workforce procrastinates' (Darius Foroux, 17 June 2019), https://dariusforoux.com/procrastination-study, accessed December 2025

others wait for the 'right time', hustlers make *now* their time. They act with urgency and see doors open and opportunities unfold.

REFLECTION EXERCISE

Think about your own life and career to date. Note down examples of when you have:

- **Acted with urgency:** Recognising the true value of time and acting decisively is crucial. Immediate, intentional action can set you apart.
- **Decided not to procrastinate:** Delaying action is not a temporary setback; it leads to missed opportunities and tangible losses.
- **Overcome emotional barriers:** Procrastination often stems from emotional barriers such as fear of failure or uncertainty. Confronting these feelings directly and acting despite them is essential for success.

Be persistent

Persistence is, without a doubt, one of the key things that got me to where I am today. By this, I don't just mean working hard. I mean relentlessly pushing forward, no matter what obstacles get in the way. The difference between those who make it and those who don't isn't talent, intelligence, or even luck. It's endurance; it's the ability to keep going long after most people would have quit.

I've seen it time and time again. People start something full of energy and excitement, convinced they're going to succeed. Then, the first setback hits. They lose some money, a deal falls through, something doesn't go as planned and suddenly, they're questioning everything. Instead of pushing on, they slow down, make excuses and tell themselves it's not the right time. Then, before they even realise it, they've given up completely.

Take Andy, for example. He had a great business idea for a fitness brand that he was passionate about. He set up an online store, got some initial interest, but, after a few months, sales weren't where he wanted them to be. Instead of adjusting his strategy, learning from his mistakes and doubling down, he let frustration get the better of him. He put in less and less effort, convinced himself the market was too competitive and eventually shut the business down. A year later, someone else launched a similar brand and made it work. The only thing they did differently? They stuck with it. They adapted, kept pushing and didn't let the early struggles defeat them.

Persistence is what separates the people who talk about success from the people who actually achieve it. Every successful person you see has failed at something. The difference between them and the 'failures' is they didn't let *their* failure stop them. They got up, adjusted and kept going.

Business, like life, will test you. There will be times when it feels like nothing is working, when every door seems to close and quitting feels like the easier option.

But that's when persistence matters most. There's no need for persistence when things are good. It's about pushing through the hard times, showing up even when you don't feel like it and refusing to back down just because things aren't happening as fast as you want them to.

Success doesn't come to those who try – it comes to those who *keep* trying.

REFLECTION EXERCISE

Think about your own life and career to date. Note down examples of when you have:

- **Proactively responded to a setback:** Everyone faces failures, disappointments or hurdles. The crucial thing is how you respond.
- **Shown persistence:** True success is built on the ability to relentlessly move forwards, despite obstacles and setbacks.
- **Adapted rather than quit:** When facing challenges, adapting your strategy rather than abandoning your goals helps ensure long-term success.

Be decisive

Decision making is a skill that you develop over time, not something you're born with. Like any skill, it takes practice, experience and a fair few mistakes along the way to perfect it. When you're just starting out in business you will make some bad decisions. The important thing is not to beat yourself up over it. It's part of the process.

When I first started, I made plenty of bad calls. I invested in the wrong things, trusted the wrong people and spent money where I shouldn't have. Every single one of those mistakes taught me something. Over time, you start recognising patterns, understanding risks better and making smarter choices. Good decision making isn't about getting everything right from day one, it's about learning, adjusting and improving.

A lot of people hesitate because they're scared of making the wrong decision. They overthink, delay and end up doing nothing at all. The truth is: no decision is often worse than a bad decision. At least when you make a move, you're learning, adapting and gaining experience. As with procrastination, sitting still gets you nowhere.

Let me tell you about Bec, who had always dreamed of opening her own coffee shop and finally took the plunge. She found the perfect location, invested her savings and proudly opened the doors. Initially, customers loved the cosy atmosphere and quality coffee. However, Bec soon faced decisions she hadn't anticipated. Should she expand her menu to include hot food? Should she start marketing online more aggressively? Competitors nearby were introducing loyalty programmes, should she follow suit? Instead of taking swift, decisive action, Bec hesitated. She spent days, then weeks, researching every option, hoping the right choice would become obvious. She feared making mistakes, convinced a single wrong decision could ruin everything. Meanwhile, her competitors acted quickly, introducing popular new offerings, attracting a good chunk of her market. Inevitably, sales dropped as customers began drifting away, drawn to more dynamic cafes. The business became unsustainable and closed less than a year after opening. The ultimate failure of Bec's business wasn't due to her making the wrong decision, it was down to her inability to make any decision at all.

As you grow in business, your decision-making ability will sharpen. You'll start trusting your instincts, making calls with more confidence and knowing when to take risks and when to hold back. It's not something anyone can teach you in a textbook (although I can offer you some tips), you have to live it, go through it and pick up the lessons as you go.

REFLECTION EXERCISE

Think about your own life and career to date. Note down examples of when you have:

- **Made a quick decision:** In fast-moving industries, slow decision making can give your competitors the edge. Decisiveness allows you to keep pace and be agile in response to change – your instincts sharpen, your confidence builds and your ability to assess risk improves.

- **Admitted that you've made a mistake:** The goal isn't perfection – it's progression. With increased confidence from practising and building your

decision-making skills, you'll be able to hold your hands up and admit where you've gone wrong.
- **Changed a decision or direction:** Every wrong decision offers a valuable lesson. Learning from poor choices in the past helps you make better ones in the future.

Self-confidence

Self-confidence is something you need by the bucket load in this game. Unfortunately, it is something you probably won't have much of when you first start out in business. And that's normal. When you're new to the hustle, it's hard to fully trust your instinct because, let's face it, you don't have much experience yet. You second-guess yourself, look for reassurance from others and sometimes even go against your gut because you assume other people must know better.

I've made this mistake myself. There were times when I ignored my own judgement and was guided by what someone else told me, purely because I was young and maybe a bit green, but mostly because I didn't have the confidence to trust my own thinking. More often than not, I ended up regretting it. While advice can be helpful, nobody sees the full picture the way you do. No one else is in your exact position, dealing with your exact challenges, so even the best advice can sometimes be completely wrong for you.

I learned, again the hard way, that nobody knows better than you when it comes to your business. You shouldn't rely on anyone but yourself. Sure, people can offer advice, and sometimes it's worth listening to, but at the end of the day, the final call is yours. If you don't learn to back yourself early on, you'll end up constantly looking for outside validation instead of making bold moves on your own terms.

This is not to say you should ignore everything and everyone, and act like you know it all from day one. That's arrogance, not confidence. What I'm saying is, take things on board, listen to people who have experience, but don't let outside voices drown out your own instincts. The more decisions you make, the more you learn. And the more you learn, the more confident you'll become.

Like a lot of these entrepreneurial skills, self-confidence in business isn't something you're just born with. It's something that develops over time. Every mistake you make, every win you secure, every decision you see play out, will all build up your ability to trust yourself. Once you start trusting your own judgement, you really start making progress.

Initially, though, you'll have to keep it simple. Prioritise what matters, put your time into the most important tasks and don't get caught up in the small stuff. Because the more efficiently you manage your time, the faster you'll move forward.

REFLECTION EXERCISE

Think about your own life and career to date. Note down examples of when you have:

- **Trusted your instincts:** Your own gut instinct is invaluable because your unique perspective matters more than anyone else's opinion.
- **Acted when you were uncertain:** Confidence grows from doing, getting things wrong, adjusting and learning. Each decision you make sharpens your judgement and belief in yourself.
- **Learned on the job:** Sometimes the only way to learn is to jump in; you don't know what you don't know yet.

A lot of people say they're ambitious. They talk about their big goals, their dreams and the lifestyle they want, but that doesn't necessarily mean they are a hustler. The difference? Someone with ambition wants success. A hustler *makes it happen*. I've seen it first-hand – the people who have ambition but never seem to get anywhere, versus the ones who actually do something about it. Having big dreams is great, but without action, they mean nothing.

Hopefully, after reading this, you are a little more convinced that you've got what it takes. Now you need to prove it, by coming up with an idea and running with it.

So, are you content with merely dreaming, or are you a hustler who is ready to get stuck in?

2
Finding An Idea That Works

From a young age, I had one clear dream: to be a footballer. This wasn't just an idle pipedream either. I was good enough to get scouted by both Millwall and Charlton on the same day. I chose Charlton because they were in the Premiership at the time, and it felt like I'd made it. Then life threw me a harsh curveball. Aged just fifteen, I was diagnosed with osteomyelitis, an infection in my bones and a common variable immune deficiency. My life's dream was shattered in an instant. Suddenly, I found myself off the pitch, a teenager with a future rewritten. Not only had I lost all passion for sport overnight, but I also had to rethink my career from scratch.

I was gutted, of course, but I didn't waste time drowning in regret. Instead, I asked myself: *What now?* I refused to be someone who just scraped by.

I craved more. I wanted financial freedom and a life built on my own terms. Meanwhile, always niggling away at the back of my head was the prevailing message at school that no one, especially not someone like me, should dare dream too big. I wasn't having any of that. I began scribbling down every business idea that came to mind. After watching the film *Law of Attraction*, I also started a vision board with pictures of all the things I wanted to achieve through my hard work. (So much of what was on there has come true. I have the same car as the one on the board – albeit in a different colour – and the house I live in looks the same as the one on the board.) These actions were all driven by a mindset that, if I wanted something, I needed to believe in it.

A different path

I quickly found that when you're not constantly being talked down to, or dismissed, clarity emerges and ideas start flowing. My first ventures were humble. To begin with, I produced flyers with a school friend, offering to clear gardens, move rubbish, anything really. It wasn't a runaway success, but it marked the start of something new. It also taught me some valuable first lessons about initiative, determination and resilience. I moved onto the bong business, which, as I said, initially soared and then failed almost overnight when eBay changed its policy. Another lesson well learned.

FINDING AN IDEA THAT WORKS

I had a brief flirtation with being a wage slave. Unsure where to turn next, I enrolled in a short electrical engineering course, hoping to find stability as a lift engineer. I'd been partly influenced in this choice by a friend. While he'd had a better chance of success at school than me, having gone to the local grammar, like me he didn't know what to do to realise his ambitions. Yet, when we both found ourselves working in the same industry, which neither of us particularly enjoyed, we came to different conclusions about what to do about it. Being told exactly what to do all the time really grated against me. I hated being dictated to. It was something I'd resented since school. I did something about it, and my friend stayed put.

After that, my career trajectory became a bit chaotic. I'd briefly considered becoming an electrician and then made a segue into finance after becoming intrigued by the stock market and sales. I financed my own studies, passing the initial financial exams. While I was looking for a job as a stockbroker, I landed a sales role at a carbon credits company as an interim measure. I'd been unaware that it wasn't operating – how should I say this? – ethically. While my sales skills flourished, my association with the dodgy carbon credits firm damaged my credibility when applying to be a stockbroker. I was devastated when a promising interview with a good stockbroking firm collapsed because they discovered my previous employer was blacklisted.

At this point, aged nineteen, I'd been through more jobs than a lot of people have in a lifetime. Strangely,

31

I wasn't disheartened. Quite the opposite. I was surer than ever that I wanted to go it alone and start my own business. As well as cultivating a mindset that was better able to overcome fear, uncertainty and doubt, my experiences thus far also meant I knew a whole lot about a large number of different industries. That, as I would discover, would stand me in good stead when coming up with ideas for future business ventures.

To keep myself solvent, I went back to sales, this time selling industrial printers. It wasn't my dream, but it was a job to keep me going while I came up with my next business idea. There, I met Matt, a colleague who, like me, aspired to something bigger. He'd previously worked at a training company and what he told me led me to see an opportunity we could pursue. Together we started Trusted Training 4U, my first properly structured business venture.

Our concept was straightforward: we provided mandatory training courses – like first aid, fire marshal training and health and safety – to companies across the country. It was simple but effective. We hired freelance trainers nationwide, handled the scheduling remotely and charged businesses a daily fee, pocketing a decent margin each time. The business grew quickly. In a short space of time, we expanded our trainer network, opened an office and hired staff. This was the first in what was to be many entrepreneurial ventures for me.

The path to setting up your own business isn't always clear or conventional, but with determination and a willingness to learn from every mistake, you can build a future that's truly your own.

Where the ideas come from

Ideas for businesses won't just fall into your lap. They come from being plugged in, constantly researching and paying attention to where the world is heading. You need to study markets, watch trends and surround yourself with the right people.

The world around you

For me, ideas are everywhere. I get them from watching and listening to podcasts, following industry leaders, analysing emerging markets and spotting gaps before everyone else does. Some people's approach is to look at what's working right now, but I'm always looking at what's going to work *next*. Where is the money flowing? What industries are about to explode? Who's solving problems in new ways?

A great example of this is the rise of digital finance. Everything money related is moving online – payments, investing, banking, even currencies. Traditional finance is being disrupted, and I saw the wave coming. That's why I started a fintech company that processes payments. I knew that the shift wasn't just likely, it was inevitable. When you understand where the world is going, you can position yourself ahead of the curve instead of chasing trends once they're already mainstream.

Business is about timing. If you can spot what's coming before everyone else does, you're already ahead of 90% of people. That's what the hustle mindset is all about: being relentless in your research, staying ahead of the trends and never waiting for opportunities to come to you. You have to see them, chase them and create them.

The people around you

But it's not just about research, it's also about who you surround yourself with. Ideas don't just come from reading reports or crunching numbers; they come from conversations, networking and being in the right rooms.

The people I spend time with are entrepreneurs, investors and forward-thinkers. They're constantly talking about what's next, what's broken and what opportunities are out there. The more you seek out those people and immerse yourself in those discussions, the more you start connecting the dots that others don't even see yet.

Innovate, don't invent

An important thing to understand is that you are not looking for something 100% original. A totally new idea is hugely rare. In fact, it barely ever happens. All you need to come up with is an innovation, not an invention.

Take cars as an example. Every major car brand is in a constant race to innovate and improve. They are not trying to create a new product altogether. Cars already exist, and do a great job of getting us from A to B. Instead, manufacturers focus on making them faster, safer, more efficient or more luxurious. Another example is smartphones. Apple, Samsung and other companies aren't creating entirely new concepts every year. They're refining and innovating on what already exists. It's the same with the business you are going to start. Being innovative isn't about being the first, it's about being the best. Instead of worrying about whether something already exists, I focus on how I can improve, refine and outperform the existing offering. That's where real success lies.

REFLECTION EXERCISE

With the above in mind, think of an industry you are interested in and answer the following questions:

- What are the weaknesses in the products/services currently on sale?
- When people talk about these products/services, what do they complain about? What are the pain points?
- As a user of the product/service, what would you change about the user experience?
- Is there potential for AI, automation, blockchain or fintech innovations to be applied to this industry to create something fresh?

Once you know what is holding existing companies back, you can work on building a business that addresses the main issues. I'll give you an example. Let's say I wanted to enter the e-commerce space to sell dog accessories. Instead of wasting time trying to come up with a brand-new product, I'd look at successful brands and analyse their weaknesses to find opportunities:

- If customers are complaining about slow shipping, I'd focus on fast delivery.
- If they're complaining about poor communication, I'd invest heavily in customer service.
- If they're frustrated about poor product quality, I'd ensure my supplier and manufacturing process are top tier.
- If reviews mention confusing or outdated websites, I'd prioritise a clean, user-friendly online store with seamless checkout.
- If customers say it's hard to find the right size or product fit, I'd offer better guides, filters and return policies to reduce friction.
- If loyalty seems low or repeat purchases are rare, I'd create an incentive-driven loyalty scheme to boost retention.

The point here is that you don't need to create something completely new, you just need to do what you're doing better than everyone else.

None of the businesses I have started has been revolutionary. They've all been built by looking at what already exists, identifying the gaps and filling them. That's how you build a business that wins.

The power of trends

If you truly want to achieve financial freedom and build a business of a significant scale, you'll need to keep a close eye on trends. In our fast-paced world, trends can explode overnight, make people millionaires and then disappear just as quickly. Your goal is to spot and capitalise on them before they start that (often rapid) downwards trajectory.

Staying ahead of trends is key. You don't want to invest time, money and energy into something that's already on its way out. You need to be current, adaptable and always looking for what's next. At the same time, though, you don't want to jump in too early. If the market is not ready and no one yet 'gets it', your concept is vulnerable to failure. Once an idea has been rejected, it is almost impossible to resurrect it.

Of course, if this was easy, everyone would be doing it and we'd all be millionaires. You can give yourself an advantage by taking a strategic approach. If you're serious about business, you have to be aware of market shifts, emerging industries where opportunities are opening up. How can you do this? I'm constantly researching market investments, looking at where the big money is going. If savvy investors are pouring billions into a specific industry, it's usually for a reason. A good way to do this is to sign up to the daily email alerts offered by many businesses that service specific sectors. For example, in the tech sector, which is always evolving, Sifted sends out an alert every morning, highlighting the businesses that have secured VC investments. When I was starting my payment solutions business, I researched how much was being invested into fintech. The numbers were huge, which told me the industry had legs. At the time of writing, another big emerging trend relates to energy mis-selling, a scandal similar to the mis-selling of PPI but instead involves the secret commissions which have inflated the overall energy spend for businesses. It impacts every core industry sector in the UK, with some losses running into the hundreds of thousands.[3] Efforts to redress the issue are still in the early stages, but there have already been court cases and successful claims. That tells me this market is growing and there is an opportunity.

If you just want to earn a decent income and replace your salary by working for yourself, you don't necessarily need to chase trends. A solid business in a steady market can do the job. But if you're looking to build a multimillion-pound company, trends are everything. You need to be ahead of the curve,

---

3   Energy and Sustainability Solutions, 'Business Energy Claims reveals the astounding extent of energy mis-selling', *Energy and Sustainability Solutions* (20 June 2022), https://essmag.co.uk/business-energy-claims-reveals-the-astounding-extent-of-energy-mis-selling, accessed December 2025

watching for what's coming next and positioning yourself where the money is flowing to.

REFLECTION EXERCISE

Take some time to do some digging around sectors that have caught your eye. Note down three trends that you think you could build a business around.

Busting the 'passion' myth

Business books and websites are always filled with advice on how to create a category-killing idea. I don't always agree with them all. One of the biggest mistakes I hear is telling people to wait until they find something they are passionate about.

Thinking you need to build a business based on a passion is a big mistake because it provides an easy excuse to procrastinate and sit on the fence, waiting for that one perfect idea you're passionate about before you start a business. The reality of business is, passion isn't always the starting point. If your goal is financial freedom, building wealth and creating opportunities, then sometimes you just need to jump in, get involved, learn the game and figure it out as you go in a sector you might not be that interested in.

I always tell people to ask themselves: *Why am I doing this?* If your reason is to create a better life for yourself and your family and to have the freedom to never rely on a salary again, then why limit yourself to only what you're passionate about? Also, passions can evolve. I've done loads of different things over the years. Some of them, I had no interest in at all at the start. But as I built them, I became passionate about the process itself because succeeding in business is the real buzz.

If you are someone who thinks you have to find the perfect business that aligns with your interests, then you are going to be disappointed. That's not how the real world works. What if the thing you're passionate about is in a market that's already saturated? What if there's no real demand? If you go all in on something just because you like it, but there's no money in it, you'll end up frustrated and broke.

Passion is great, but progress and experience are what really matter in the beginning. Get involved, take action and let passion find you along the way. Most importantly, focus on what's profitable, where there's demand and where you can add value. Once you've learned how business works and built something from the ground up, when your finances are secure, your network is strong and you understand how to scale, you'll have the time and money to choose passion projects and chase what excites you. But at the beginning? The key is just to start.

Don't overthink it

The best advice I can give to a would-be entrepreneur struggling for business ideas is simple: stop overthinking it or trying to come up with something groundbreaking and just start the business that sounds the most plausible. As I have shown here, you don't need a revolutionary idea to start a business, you just need a concept that works.

At its core, business is about buying either something and selling it for a profit or offering a service and getting paid for your time and/or expertise. That's it. You don't need to build the next Uber or create the next big tech innovation. If you can find something to sell, whether it's a product, a service or your own skills, then you're already ahead of 99% of people who sit around waiting for the 'perfect' idea.

In the following chapter, I'll go through how to validate your ideas. For now though, a reality about entrepreneurialism: your first idea will not always be the best one you come up with. In fact, even if it sounds amazing at first, it might be terrible. Don't stop thinking of ideas once you have one, and be prepared to drop them and move on.

Also, don't be afraid of starting small. Even if it doesn't work, the knowledge you'll gain and lessons you'll learn along the way will be invaluable. For example, you'll know how to:

- Set up a company
- Work with an accountant
- Build a website
- Market a product

- Network

- Put yourself into new situations

Most importantly, you'll start meeting other business-minded people, which will help you refine your ideas and open doors to new opportunities.

Just to get you started, here are eight ideas for simple, low setup cost yet profitable small businesses you could launch right away:

1. **Freelancing:** Offer services like writing, graphic design, coding or social media management. Websites like Fiverr and Upwork make it easy to start.

2. **Reselling:** Buy discounted or second-hand items and flip them for a profit on eBay, Facebook Marketplace or Depop.

3. **Consulting/coaching:** If you have expertise in anything – fitness, marketing, finance or mindset coaching, for example – you can start charging for advice.

4. **Print-on-demand:** Create and sell custom T-shirts, mugs and posters without holding inventory through platforms like Printful or Redbubble.

5. **Local services:** Try car detailing, pressure washing, tutoring or pet sitting. Find a simple

service people need and start offering it in your area.

6. **Digital products:** Consider selling ebooks, online courses or digital templates on platforms like Gumroad or Teachable.

7. **Handmade goods:** If you're crafty, sell your creations on Etsy or at local markets. Think jewellery, art or home décor.

8. **Affiliate marketing:** Start a blog or social media channel reviewing products and earn a commission from affiliate links.

There are lots of good business ideas, but the key is to take action. Don't be like so many other would-be entrepreneurs, stuck in the planning phase, convinced they need the perfect idea, more experience or a bigger budget before they can start. Most successful hustlers succeed by doing, not by waiting. Every great business starts somewhere, often in the simplest form: selling a product online, offering a service to friends and family or turning a hobby into income. You don't need to have everything figured out, you just need to take the first step.

Once you've started, momentum will build. You'll face challenges, of course, but with every challenge comes growth. You'll develop skills, gain clarity and spot opportunities you would never have seen if you were still stuck overthinking. You don't have to get it right the first time; you just have to get going.

This is your invitation to start small, start scrappy and, most importantly, start *now*, even if you haven't quite got the 'big idea' yet. Use what you have, where you are and build as you go. Progress beats perfection every time. The only real failure is not starting at all.

3
A Reality Check: Validating Your Idea

A guy I know – let's call him Mike – came up with the idea for a cab app. It was basically another Uber or Bolt, but his idea was based on charging drivers a fraction of the percentage commission that other businesses charged.

On paper, it looked like a solid business idea. Ridesharing is a huge industry and there's always demand. Mike even managed to get some decent investment. Unfortunately, as it turned out, this was the cab app that went nowhere. A few years after coming up with the idea, no one even knows about the service, let alone has used it.

Good idea, bad business

Ultimately this is a story about how a good idea can still fail. Here's where Mike went wrong:

- **A market is dominated by giants:** Uber and Bolt have already taken over the vast bulk of ridesharing businesses. Even though there are smaller competitors, most people have never heard of them. Why? Because competing with these companies requires an insane amount of money, resources and infrastructure.

- **High setup costs:** Setting up a business like this is astronomically expensive. To even stand a chance, you need the best app, the best marketing and endless funding. The established ridesharing apps have spent billions building their brand, their tech and their driver networks. To go up against that, you'd need a war chest of money. Take marketing as an example. Operating with the tiny margins Mike was proposing is a numbers game; you need tens of thousands of bums on (taxi) seats to make it work. That means a big marketing spend.

- **Lack of know-how:** Mike didn't really know what he was doing, because he had no experience. Before this, he had owned and run a nightclub. He knew nothing at all about building a consumer app. He relied on other people to build and run the rideshare business, which is always risky. If you don't understand the business yourself, you're relying on people who may not always have your best interests in mind. You'll also make some poor decisions. For example, Mike spent £15,000 getting an app built by a firm in India. There's nothing wrong with these firms, but this was a fraction of what he should have been spending and the app was nowhere near as slick as those from the likes of Uber, who spent millions on their tech. Not even close. Plus, it required ongoing development and Mike should have been in the same room as his developers. It was never going to be as simple as just creating a pretty app.

- **Location:** Mike was based in Spain, not even close to the markets he was targeting. He's now stuck. Some years after first coming up with the idea, he's burnt through endless amounts of investor money and he's still nowhere near launching. At this point, it's unclear if the business will ever work. At the heart of the problem was that, while it was a good *idea*, it simply wasn't a viable business opportunity. If Mike had properly analysed the market, he'd have quickly realised that the challenges involved vastly outweighed the potential for success.

Viability

A viable business opportunity is something that has a realistic chance of succeeding, where the competition isn't overwhelming, the costs to compete aren't astronomical and there's a genuine gap in the market.

When you come up with your business idea, before you do anything else, you must do some market research and consider whether it is a viable business opportunity. If you've got an idea now, answer these questions before you take it any further:

1. Is there space for my business in this market? Or am I trying to compete with billion-dollar companies that already dominate?

2. What are the barriers to entry? Do I need an insane amount of money, connections or experience just to get started?

3. Can I actually compete? If I enter this space, can I genuinely offer something better than or different from what already exists?

4. How long will it be until I see results? Am I going to be tied up for years, burning through money, without making real progress?

5. Do I have the experience and knowledge I need to succeed in this space?

A viable business doesn't just look good on paper; it has a realistic chance of succeeding. Too many people chase ideas that are too expensive, too risky or have too much competition, thinking they'll be the next big thing. But unless they have unlimited resources or a truly game-changing idea, they're fighting a losing battle.

My best bad idea

When I first started out in business, market research wasn't something I paid much attention to. It wasn't that I turned a blind eye to it, I was just impulsive. I'd get excited about an idea, jump in headfirst and figure things out as I went along.

This is another of my hard-learned lessons. After experiencing some success with my training company, I decided to enter the hospitality industry, opening a franchise of a restaurant called ISO Sushi in Sidcup. A big part of why I did it was that I had always dreamed of owning a restaurant and thought I had a good idea. But success in this space isn't just about the concept, it's about building something that can stand on its own.

If you launch a business solely because you love the idea, you risk overlooking the daily grind of managing costs, marketing, operations and unforeseen setbacks. When your focus is only on the product or service, you limit your potential. You must be prepared to tackle every aspect of that business, even those parts you'd rather avoid, and if you don't know how, you need the determination to learn quickly.

Looking back, my biggest mistake with the sushi restaurant was jumping in too fast. I saw what I thought was a promising opportunity, got encouragement from a friend and, driven by a fear of missing out, I said, 'Let's do it.' I secured a small space, set up the kitchen and had the restaurant up and running in seven months, after having grossly underestimated the work and cost involved. In my haste, I overlooked critical details. I didn't thoroughly research the local market and the demographics of the potential customer base, then quickly discovered that the competition was a lot fiercer than I had anticipated and not as many people in the area as I'd hoped were keen on sushi.

When you launch something new, the first few months will usually go well – people like trying new things – but that can quite easily drop off. This was exactly what happened to my restaurant. Very quickly, we found ourselves struggling to generate the long-lasting revenue needed to keep the business afloat.

That experience taught me a hard lesson: if you're going to build something from scratch, you need to lean on cold, hard data and have a clear target for your marketing. Before you take the plunge, you must understand your industry inside out, validate your timing and learn to recognise the red flags of bad ideas. How? With market research.

Market research

It took a lot of time and money for me to learn just how important market research is, but now I know it is non-negotiable. If you don't do your groundwork, you're setting yourself up to fail. Launching a successful business isn't just about having deep pockets. It's about making smart, creative moves when resources are tight. It's about meticulous planning and being ready to adapt every step of the way.

If you learn how to harness data, you will be able to truly understand an industry before you dive in and can ignore the misleading signals that can push you toward doomed ventures. With careful planning and a willingness to learn from every misstep, you can build something lasting, even when you're starting with very little.

Vision is what drives entrepreneurs forward and keeps them pushing even when things aren't going their way. Yet, having a vision doesn't mean blindly running with the first idea that pops into your head. You've still got to do your research. You need to look into the market, trends and timing to find out if your vision is something that can actually happen right now, or if you are chasing an idea that's either outdated or too ahead of its time. That's where a lot of people go wrong. They have a vision, but they don't stop to check if it's the right vision at the right moment.

Developing a product or service without ensuring there's a genuine market need is one of the most common pitfalls that derails new businesses. It's tempting to assume that because you find an idea exciting, others will too. However, skipping the market research stage can see you investing time and resources into something that ultimately doesn't resonate with potential customers. You might be familiar with the statistic that nearly half of businesses fail within the first five years, but did you know that 35% of start-ups fail because there is no market demand?[4] The rule of thumb here is to engage with your target audience early, gather feedback and be prepared to pivot based on their actual needs.

What should you be looking at when conducting market research, and how do you go about it? I've already explained that I watch podcasts, read reports and follow market trends to see where opportunities are heading, but you need to go further than this when interrogating specific ideas. Getting sufficient market research requires a multistage approach. To explain it properly, I will use the example of 'Danny'.

Danny runs a boxing gym and has a sideline as a personal trainer. Danny works all hours. On a typical day, he will begin training at 6am and not leave until 6pm, having trained back-to-back clients. He loves his job but thinks there may be a better way to make a living. What, he wonders, about creating his own range of branded boxing gloves? To verify whether this could be a viable business, I would suggest he works through the following steps:

1. Understand demand

2. Competitor analysis

---

4   R McMillan, 'What percentage of businesses fail and why?' (Capsule, 12 July 2024), https://capsulecrm.com/blog/what-percentage-of-businesses-fail, accessed December 2024

3. Check the financials

4. Brainstorm the idea

Let's dig into each of these steps in detail.

Understand demand

Before doing anything, it is crucial that Danny finds out if there is a market for branded boxing gloves. He needs an idea of how many people might want to buy a pair of boxing gloves in any one day. If it is just one person, that's not a lucrative market, especially for a brand no one has ever heard of. That one person is far more likely to buy a more well-known, even leading brand. If, however, two thousand or more people are in the market for boxing gloves each day, there is potential space for a new player with a head for marketing. How, though, do you find out if there is one potential customer or two thousand?

Most people's first port of call when buying anything is to search for it online. In this case, they'll almost certainly type 'boxing gloves' into Google. If you can find out how many searches there are for the item, service or problem per day, this will give you a clue about the level of demand. There's a great piece of software called SEMrush that can show you how many times a keyword is searched for. I searched 'boxing gloves' and saw that there were nearly 19,000 searches for them in one month, which would indicate a fairly healthy market. But it can give you even more information than this. For example, my search for boxing gloves revealed that the two largest markets for these items are in the US and UK. There is also a seasonality to boxing glove sales, with people seeming to be keener on the sport in the summer months. This means there will be spikes in demand that Danny will need to account for.

The search will also reveal your 'keyword difficulty' (KD), which indicates how difficult it will be to drive his boxing gloves up the rankings and appear higher up in the search results. A high KD – say, 75% – means it would be very hard for Danny to get his boxing gloves to rank highly on Google, which means potential customers will find it difficult to discover them through searching online.

A great business idea isn't just about having a good product; you need to know that it's possible to get that product in front of the right audience. If you can dominate the space with the right digital strategy, that's a huge advantage.

If Danny is prepared to refine his product, he can adjust the search by adding keyword variations to see if there might be demand for a specific type of glove. He could try various options, such as:

- 'Best boxing gloves for beginners'
- 'Cheap boxing gloves UK'
- 'Boxing gloves for women'

This might uncover a previously untapped, or undervalued market. There is an element of risk here

A REALITY CHECK: VALIDATING YOUR IDEA

though: it might be untapped for a reason. If people aren't searching for it, there might be no demand. If there's no demand, it's a waste of time. More research will be required before jumping into something like this. But if the numbers show a clear market and, better yet, there appears to be a gap that others aren't filling or getting quite right, you'll know you're onto something.

Competitor analysis

If the market looks promising – in this case, let's assume it did – Danny can then go back to Google and do a general search to see which other companies are doing well in the boxing gloves space. Which are the top brands and what are they offering? To avoid his own search history and personalisation skewing the results, he should open an 'incognito' or private browsing window, which will give a more neutral view of the search engine results pages (SERPs).

Danny could start with his 'boxing glove' search, but then expand it with terms such as:

- 'Buy boxing gloves online'
- 'Boxing gloves UK'
- 'Boxing gloves under £50'

For each search, he should note which brands keep popping up at the top of the results. It's also useful to look at the type of content. Is it, for example, e-commerce stores selling boxing gloves, or review sites, or blogs? Likewise, what kind of pages rank highly? Is it product pages, listicles or YouTube videos? This shows both who is dominating the market and also what kind of content Google favours. He should then check out the paid ads at the top and bottom of the page; are they for big brands like Everlast and Adidas, or are the smaller, niche brands paying to play? If it's the latter, this shows that the bids for ad space are not too aggressive, so there is room for Danny to give his content a paid push.

One of the main goals of the competitor analysis is to see if you can do it better. Is there a gap that everyone else is missing? There are a few ways to look into this. To start with, I would have a good dig around the websites of the biggest players, exploring their product ranges, what sort of delivery terms they offer (free delivery, bundles or subscription) and seeing whether they collect emails for marketing. Are these sites slick, fast and mobile-friendly, or do they plod along? This is all useful intel and helps to identify any gaps that you can fill.

The second way to approach this, and something I always find useful, is to see what people are saying about the brands already on the market. Check out their Google and/or TrustPilot reviews. Read the best and worst reviews to see what people think about the competition. Even without looking, I can say with some certainty that, for Danny's market, customer service will be a big discussion point.

For the majority of online retailers, it is always bad customer service that riles shoppers. Since big brands handed everything over to bots, customer service has definitely taken a turn for the worse. A lot of companies don't even publish a contact number or email address anymore. Don't get me wrong, I love technology, but it is great to have a human presence too. If you find that customer service is a real issue, this is a big opportunity. Similarly, check out the social media presence of the competition. If their timelines are filled with complaints and they are not particularly engaged with it, this speaks volumes.

Later on, if and when you come to start developing your product, look at the Google Shopping and Image results. This is a quick and easy way to check popular price points, common colours and styles and the most used types of packaging. If the visual presentation of your product is important, you need to know what's popular.

Check the financials

Even if an idea looks promising, there is one step you cannot afford to miss – literally. If the businesses in your proposed sector are not making any money, the odds are high that you won't either. It's not completely out of the question, especially if you can come up with a better model, but you need to understand the financials before you go any further.

In the UK, Companies House is a great resource and completely free to use. This is the government's official register of companies where, by typing in a competitor's name, you can find out their:

- Turnover and revenue
- Profit and loss
- Assets and liabilities
- Directors and shareholders

Small, or 'micro', companies might file abridged accounts, in which case the figures will be limited, but still useful for comparison.

It can be an interesting exercise to go back a few years to see how the players in this sector have grown – or not. If you dig around a bit more, you may also be able to find a valuation.

For more detailed financial breakdowns, there are some premium (ie paid-for) tools that give deeper insights. This is worth doing if you are serious about the business. Such sources include:

- Endole: Revenue, credit scores, ownership structure (some info is free)
- Beauhurst: Especially good for high-growth or funded UK companies
- FullCircl: For B2B and credit risk research
- Creditsafe/Red Flag Alert: Useful for quick revenue and credit data

A REALITY CHECK: VALIDATING YOUR IDEA

Some of these services may require free sign-up, or offer a few reports at no cost.

If a competitor sells on Amazon, there are also options for checking marketplace rankings, and you can find estimates of monthly sales volumes and pricing based on listings. Try Jungle Scout, Helium 10 or Keepa.

Finally – and this might sound a bit old school, but it works – speak to people in the industry. For our example, Danny could ask around among suppliers, or boxing glove wholesalers, about who is moving the most product and which brands are doing the best right now. These people are also a great source of constructive feedback.

Brainstorm the idea

One of my final and most important steps is to stress test my ideas with people I am close to. You need to choose carefully and only rely on those whose opinions you trust, not just anyone, because getting feedback from the wrong people can be worse than no feedback at all. If someone isn't in business, doesn't understand trends or isn't forward-thinking, their opinion isn't going to help me refine my idea. We've all got friends who will say something is terrible just to wind you up; or friends in steady 9–5 jobs who can't understand why anyone would want to start a business, so won't be all that encouraging even if your idea is out of this world. I bounce ideas off other entrepreneurs and industry experts. These are people I trust and who think big, know markets and can give me real, actionable insights.

For example, I always run my ideas by Poppy McMillan, who was once my employee and is now my business partner. If she thinks something hasn't got a chance, she'll be honest and say so and, likewise, she tells me when something sounds interesting. Sometimes, a simple conversation can lead to a breakthrough. When you have to explain your idea to someone else, it is an opportunity to step back, break ideas down, and properly analyse what's missing in the market: *What are the pain points? What are competitors doing wrong? Where can I do it better?* The best business ideas aren't just about competing; they're about adding value in a way no one else is.

Just as a footnote to Danny's story, he did speak with me about it and I thought it was a good idea, based on the research he'd done. In fact, I became an investor. The business is called Bellwether Boxing & Fitness.

Coming up with a solid business idea isn't about having a random lightbulb moment; it's about putting in the work, doing the research and making sure the idea actually has legs. I don't just jump into something because it sounds good. Every idea I pursue has to be validated; that means digging deep into the market, testing demand and figuring out where I can bring real value.

Market research is what separates impulse decisions from smart business moves. If you skip it,

A REALITY CHECK: VALIDATING YOUR IDEA

you're relying on guesswork. But if you do it properly, you're making calculated moves with a higher chance of success.

Demand, competition, financials and constructive feedback – only once you have all this key information to hand will you know whether it is worth thinking about this idea seriously and taking it to the next stage. Once you know you're heading in the right direction, that's when you fully commit. That's when you block out distractions, focus and go all in. Anyone can have a vision, but only a few people actually take the time to refine, test and make it happen.

If you put the work in at the start, you won't just generate ideas – you'll generate *winning* ideas. That's what separates hustlers.

4
No Excuses, Just Action: How To Stop Overthinking And Start Doing

Great ideas are nothing without execution. When you're starting a business, speed beats perfection every time. Too many people get caught up in setting up a company and trying to make every little detail flawless. They spend months tweaking their logo, fine-tuning their website or getting a stack of crisp business cards, but the truth is, none of that matters if you never actually *make* the product.

In the next chapter, we'll look at the early versions of your product you need to make to test it out – the minimum viable product, or MVP – but first we'll talk about the stuff that should be going on in the background. 'In the background' is key here. These are the things that you should be doing at the same time as making your MVP, but not using as an excuse not to build the actual product.

Momentum

First, a word on momentum. You're not going to get everything right straight away, and that's OK. No one does. Businesses aren't built in theory; they're built in the real world, through actions, mistakes and adjustments. The faster you get going and producing what it is you are hoping to sell, the quicker you can make those mistakes, learn from them and adapt. That's how you build something real.

Taking imperfect action is one of the most powerful things you can do. You'll learn faster, you'll adapt quicker and you'll stay ahead of the people still sitting around debating their next move while creating a SWOT analysis. The hustle mindset is about execution, adjusting as you go and figuring things out in real-time. If you're waiting for the 'right moment', which you're thinking will come after you finish your business plan, you'll be waiting forever.

When you delay, or procrastinate with less important tasks, it isn't just delaying the moment that you'll actually begin to make money, it's making it less likely that you will. The longer you sit there overthinking, the more time your competitors have to move ahead of you. I've lost count of how many people have told me about a great idea they've had, only to see someone else launch it six months later because they wasted time 'planning' and focusing on all the peripheral stuff that supports the business but doesn't earn any money. The world won't wait for you to be ready. While you're fine-tuning your website landing page, they're out there getting customers, testing ideas and bringing in cash. That's why speed is everything in the beginning. Once you have got something out there, you can improve as you go.

I'm not suggesting being reckless, but momentum matters more than a perfect plan. The best time to act on your business idea is right now. Not tomorrow, not next week – now.

Hustle mindset tips to overcome procrastination

- **Create active urgency:** Treat your idea like it's time-sensitive, because it is. If you don't move fast, someone else will. Set deadlines for yourself, even if no one's holding you accountable. Speed matters.
- **Just get it done:** It's a simple but crucial point. If something needs doing, don't push it to tomorrow. Break big tasks into smaller ones and start ticking them off. Action creates momentum.
- **Don't worry about perfection:** Seeking perfection is an excuse to delay. Your first version won't be your final version, and that's fine. Launch fast, fix as you go.
- **Make decisions quickly:** Successful entrepreneurs don't sit on decisions for weeks. If you have enough information to make an educated guess, make the call and adjust later if needed.
- **Use the 'five-second rule':** If you have an idea or know you need to do something, act within five seconds before doubt creeps in. Write that email,

make that call, register that company – whatever it is, move.
- **Set non-negotiables:** Make a list of key actions you must complete every day. Non-negotiable tasks keep you disciplined and stop you from getting lost in pointless busywork.
- **Surround yourself with doers, not talkers:** Energy is contagious. If you're around people who make things happen, you'll naturally do the same. Avoid people who talk about ideas but never execute.

Let's look now at which tasks *are* worth doing in the early stages, when you should do them and how much time you should spend on them.

Business plan

Check out any start-up website, and a business plan will be up there, front and centre. Business plans are useful, and you do need one – but they are not the be-all and end-all, especially if they become the excuse that anchors you in the planning phase. Many people believe they have to have absolutely everything mapped out before they can launch their business. The truth? No matter how much you plan, or how many spreadsheets you create, you'll never feel completely ready. There's always going to be some level of uncertainty. The only way to figure things out is to get going.

NO EXCUSES, JUST ACTION

I'm not advocating going in blind. In the previous chapter, I set out just how important it was to validate your idea before doing anything. But you've done that now, so you can move onto the next stage; you don't need to keep going back to the research, 'just to check your assumptions'. If it looked good to go when you did it, it is good to go. Once you've confirmed that your idea has legs, it's time to start moving.

Write a business plan. It will give you structure. It forces you to think through your idea fully, understand your market and it gives you a roadmap. But this should be done concurrently with all the other things you need to do to get the business off the ground, not before. Don't let your focus be on writing a fifty-page plan. A basic roadmap is helpful – you need to know what you're doing and why – but don't get so caught up in writing about it that you never actually do any of the things you're planning.

Your business plan needs to be fluid, not set in stone. In the real world, things change, constantly. A lot of people treat business plans like some kind of sacred text that they must follow to the letter. The reality is, most business plans go out the window once you start. You'll hit unexpected hurdles, new opportunities will come up and you'll probably find better ways of doing things as you go.

Think of it like this: you can map out every detail of a road trip, but the second you hit traffic, get a flat tyre, or find a better route, your plan changes. Business is no different. The real world is unpredictable and the only way to succeed is to adapt.

Once you've written your plan, use it as a guide, not a rigid rulebook. It's something to get you started and keep you focused, but it should be flexible and adapt as your business evolves. What matters more than the plan itself is your ability to execute, pivot when necessary and keep moving forward. Take practical, low-risk steps that get you moving right now. Remember, what you need most is momentum.

Build the foundations

You'll need to get going with all the background structure you will need to run a company, but you have to do everything at once. Just get the basics in motion. While you're writing the business plan, set up your limited company. That's step one, because you'll need it to open a business bank account. Opening a bank account is the next step, so you can start handling transactions.

Even if you are a long way from being ready to launch, you should already be thinking about spreading the word. Marketing is so important, particularly for new businesses that no one has yet heard of. Make sure you register the business names on all the usual platforms such as Instagram, TikTok and Facebook, and buy all the domains that go with the name. Start to build up followers by posting relevant content.

Once you've done that, you can start working on your sales platform. If you are planning on selling direct online, you could start off on Etsy or even a

Website-building tools

Website builder	Best for	Advantages	Free plan includes	How to start
Wix	Total beginners, creative freedom, drag and drop design	User-friendly Lots of templates App marketplace	Wix-branded domain (eg yoursite.wixsite.com)	1. Go to www.wix.com 2. Sign up for a free account 3. Choose a template, or let AI build one for you 4. Drag, drop, edit, publish
WordPress	Blogging, content-driven sites, SEO-friendly platforms	Easy to set up Scalable	WordPress subdomain (eg yoursite.wordpress.com)	1. Visit www.wordpress.com 2. Create a free account 3. Choose a theme 4. Start adding pages, posts and media
Carrd	Simple one-page websites, personal profiles, landing pages	Fast setup Slick designs Mobile-friendly	Carrd-branded subdomain (eg yoursite.carrd.co)	1. Visit card.co 2. Choose a template 3. Customise text/images 4. Hit publish – done in ten minutes tops
Google Sites	Simple internal business sites, team pages, quick MVP	Integrates well with Google Drive No ads	Google subdomain or link from your Gmail account	1. Go to Google Sites 2. Click '+ blank site' 3. Use the editor to add text, images and files 4. Publish with one click

Facebook platform. Shopify is another good option. Alternatively, you could build your own website. You've got two options here, either building it yourself or outsourcing to a web developer. I recommend doing it yourself. At this stage, you don't need a super fancy website. You're still at the 'testing the water' stage. Build it yourself using free or low-cost tools, and you can always upgrade it later.

All of these sites are easy to use, just drag and drop images and text using the templates available. Even if you are not very tech-minded, you can't really go wrong.

You will also need to think about payment platforms, to accept money from all your new customers. The main ones to consider are summarised in the table below.

Payment platforms

Payment platform	Best for	Advantages	Best for
Stripe	Start-ups, marketplaces and custom checkouts	Developer friendly. Easy to integrate with websites and mobile apps. Handles subscriptions and one-off payments	Full control over your checkout. When building a product that scales. Selling globally
PayPal	Freelancers, solopreneurs, digital goods	Easy to set up, just link your email. Brand recognition and trust. Buyer protection and dispute support	When you're starting quickly and need a trusted solution. International sales. Invoicing clients

Square	In person sales, food trucks, retail	Hardware and software in one system	Taking payments at events or pop-ups
		Free point-of-sale (POS) app	Service-based businesses working on- and offline
		Handles appointment, stock, receipts	
Shopify Payments	E-commerce businesses on Shopify	Seamless integration with Shopify	Businesses using Shopify
		Allows Apple Pay, Google Pay and local methods	Fast setup
Wise	International freelancers, agencies, contractors	Low FX rates	Working with international clients
		Supports multiple currencies and local bank accounts	Multi-currency accounts
GoCardless	Recurring payments, B2B services, subscriptions	Focuses on Direct Debit payments (good for lower fees)	Billing clients monthly
			Avoiding card fees
		Useful for UK/EU services with repeat clients	

Prioritising

Reading this, you may well be getting a sinking feeling, thinking, *Where do I start?* The key is to work out which tasks are most critical. A simple rule of thumb is: if it doesn't directly help you launch, sell or grow, it's not important yet.

All businesses vary, so I can't give you a definitive list of exactly what to do and in what order, but fancy business cards are not what gets a business off the ground. Just bear in mind that it is easy to waste time on the wrong things, and you shouldn't stress over fine-tuning a website that no one's even visiting yet.

The three things that do really matter in the beginning are:

1. **Getting your first customers:** Whether it's cold outreach, social media or word of mouth, making your first sale is proof that people actually want what you're offering.

2. **Testing your offer:** Your first version won't be perfect, but it doesn't need to be. Launch, learn and then tweak.

3. **Creating momentum:** Once you start moving, keep moving. Consistency wins.

Everything else is just noise at this stage. The easiest way to work through the noise and work out what really counts is to break it down. In the table below I've imagined that I'm setting up a business selling colourful socks, and have written a list of some of the tasks I might think I need to get done. I've then added questions to check whether or not they should be a priority:

Priority tasks

Task	Does this help me launch faster?	Does this help me make money?	Does this help me directly improve my product or service?
Design logo	Yes	Yes	Yes
Set up website	Yes	Yes	Yes
Write an 'about' page	No	No	No
Set up a payment system	Yes	Yes	No
Set up as a ltd company	Yes	Yes	No
Build social media presence	Yes	Yes	No
Set up email marketing platform	No	Yes	No
Order business cards	No	No	No
Create pricing page	Yes	Yes	Yes
Write blog posts	No	No	No

Tables like this help you to focus on what is most important and must get done right away.

Now try it for your own business. Create your own table for the long list of tasks that are currently flooding your mind and make an honest assessment of which are genuinely necessary and urgent.

If, after doing this exercise, you have several urgent tasks, break them down into bite-sized, no-excuse steps. If something feels too overwhelming to start, that's a sign you haven't simplified it enough.

Let's say you need a website. What's the first step? Probably buying a domain. Then, you'd need to set up a simple landing page. Then you'd need to write some copy. Suddenly, 'build a website' isn't so overwhelming; it's just a checklist to work through.

Think about which actionable step you can take right now to move the business forward. Then do it.

Fear and uncertainty

Let's talk about fear and uncertainty, because, let's face it, what you are about to do feels like a pretty big deal. And it is. If you are hesitating, it's almost certain that these emotions are playing a big role. The fear of failure can be paralysing. It leads people to overthink, procrastinate and make excuses to themselves that they are 'waiting for the right moment' when, really, they're just scared of messing up.

You can't 'manage' fear. What you can do, though, is face it, move through it and *use* it. Fear isn't a stop sign; it's a signal that you're stepping into something bigger than yourself. That's exactly where you need to be if you want to succeed.

Get comfortable with the fact that you're going to fail. Then, instead of being afraid of it, focus on what you'll learn from it. Every mistake is data. Every setback is a lesson. Every time you mess up, you're a step closer to getting it right.

To show you that you don't need to fear failure, I'll share the story of another of my businesses, one where a whole bunch of things went wrong, but I used them to propel me forward and build a stronger business.

The venture in question was called Wet Paws Dartford, a dog swimming business. People would bring along their dogs and pay £40 for a thirty-minute swim session: five minutes to get the dog ready, twenty minutes in the water, then five minutes to dry off. A minute of swimming is equivalent to a mile of walking for a dog, so it's win–win for dog and owner.

The idea for the business came, as many do, out of a conversation. My friend Kelly rang me up one afternoon and told me about this place where she'd taken her dog swimming. It wasn't fancy, but it was fully booked weeks ahead. Dogs were getting fitter, happier and less destructive at home and people were paying for it.

That was the lightbulb moment. I thought, *This is it. There's demand. I'll make it better, cleaner, slicker. I'll do it right.*

By the following Monday, I'd already found a plot of land, ordered two giant pools and was working through the logistics. I was fired up, motivated and totally unprepared. This is when reality hit. What had seemed like a simple setup turned into one of the hardest projects I've done. The challenges emerged immediately:

- The ground wasn't level. I hadn't even thought about this. When the pools arrived and we tried to set them up, they were completely unstable. I had to bring in scaffolders to level it all out, which delayed everything.

- The water turned green after we filled the pools, because we didn't know what we were doing. We had to drain them and learn about proper pool maintenance. This meant hiring pool specialists to teach us about chemicals, chlorine and filtration systems.

- Setting up the booking system took time. We used Aucity, a booking system I had no experience of and integrated it with Stripe for payments, which I hadn't used in years. I had to figure out how to use them properly and it took a while to get right.

- There were legal and insurance issues. When you are dealing with people's treasured pets, insurance is essential. We had to create terms and conditions, making sure everything was legally sound.

From idea to execution, Wet Paws Dartford took two months to open, not the few weeks I'd originally thought. The key lessons? Nothing is as simple as it seems on paper and, however good something sounds, things will go wrong.

Turning a vague idea into a real business is 100% possible, but it takes more than just enthusiasm. You have to be ready for setbacks, delays and problems you've never even considered. If you expect it to be easy, you'll be in for a shock. You will screw up. You will make bad decisions. You will have days when you think, *What the hell am I doing?* Every thought will seem to come with a question mark: *Will this idea work? Will people buy what I'm selling? Will I make enough money to survive? Can I actually do this?* You won't have clear answers, and that freaks a lot of people out. They want security and guarantees, a safety net. But business doesn't come with a safety net. It's a free fall and the only way you survive is by learning how to land on your feet, over and over again. That's part of the game.

Fear serves no purpose here. If you stay committed, keep learning and adapt to the challenges as they come, you *can* take an idea and turn it into a real, profitable business.

> **Hustle mindset tips for handling fear and uncertainty**
>
> - **Trust your ability to figure things out:** You're not going to have all the answers at the start – no one does. But what separates successful entrepreneurs from everyone else is their ability to adapt. When problems arise, they don't freeze. They don't wait for someone to tell them what to do. They find solutions. If you can develop that mindset, where you trust yourself to handle whatever comes next, uncertainty stops being a problem. It just becomes part of the job.
> - **Control what you can control:** You can't predict the market, or customer behaviour, or every challenge that's going to hit you. What you can control is your effort, discipline and ability to keep moving no matter what. Focus on that.

> If you're constantly taking action, you're always in a position to adjust when things change. If you just sit there waiting for certainty, you're done before you've even started.
>
> - **Get used to chaos:** When you're the boss, everything falls on you. In business, the early stages are messy. You'll be putting out fires daily, juggling a hundred things at once and trying to keep everything from falling apart. That's normal. The sooner you accept that nothing will ever be perfectly stable, the easier it gets to handle the chaos. Instead of panicking, you'll learn to thrive in it.

Fear and uncertainty are part of being an entrepreneur. The people who win aren't the ones who have everything figured out from day one and never feel scared. They're the ones who keep moving, adapting and showing up even when they don't have all the answers.

If you want certainty, get a nine-to-five. If you want success, learn to live with the unknown and to rely on yourself.

5
Testing Ideas At Lightning Speed – The Value Of An MVP

A few years ago, I owned a gym. Like a lot of such places, it was more than just a place to work out, it was a hub. People came, stayed, chatted and, as it turned out, brought opportunities in and out every day. One of those people was Jane.

Jane worked at our front desk. She was friendly, switched on, reliable, the kind of person you're always glad to have around. When she suddenly handed in her notice one day, we were a bit stumped. There was no warning, no drama, she was just gone. A few weeks later, we found out why. She'd started something called findom. If you are not familiar with it, it is a niche platform in the adult space focused on financial domination. At the time, I knew absolutely nothing about it. But what I could quickly see was that Jane had spotted a gap in a market and jumped into it with both feet.

She was already making about £5k a month, which, of course, isn't bad. But some of the girls who had been doing it a while were pulling in £50–60k a month. On their own. From a Twitter account.

But here's where it gets even more interesting.

Jane told us that, despite the demand, there was no safe, dedicated payment platform for what she was doing. In fact, payment systems were a mess. Stripe doesn't accept adult businesses, so accounts were getting frozen, shut down and wiped out. Some creators were getting their money stuck in other third-party platforms. Others were compromising their safety by handing out personal details directly to clients. It was chaos, but also an opportunity.

There's a real and persistent problem with payment and processing and banking restrictions, particularly for small businesses and especially for anything considered 'high risk', which seems to be pretty much everything these days. I've heard loads of stories of traditional banks blocking transactions, freezing accounts and creating unnecessary bottlenecks. It's a nightmare for cash flow and user experience.

As luck would have it, at about the same time that I started thinking about this, I made a chance connection with someone who worked at a payment processing company. We got chatting, and he told me about a mobile-based solution that can send payment links instantly and accept payments without expensive equipment. What really got me excited was when he explained that the current generation of fintechs were mostly focused on one type of payment. A common one is hand-held terminals, where customers can tap their phones to pay for a coffee, or a takeaway. It seemed to me that there was an opportunity to go a lot further, to offer different types of payment options – for example, a lot of people I know use crypto these days.

From there, the concept grew. Why not expand it to combine payments, such as crypto, FX, loyalty schemes and more, all under one roof? This was the genesis for my payments services business, Pulsare Pay. The idea was to create a modular, all-in-one financial tech platform that would remove the need for multiple service providers, empowering users with faster, simpler and more flexible financial tools.

Of course, this was an ambitious undertaking. It wasn't something I was going to be able to launch overnight. Pulsare Pay would be complex to build, and then there was all the regulatory stuff that comes with any financial product. Plus, I needed to check if there would be demand for this payment services business. Was it solving any real pain point?

After pulling together a team, we started to explore the regulatory side and, at the same time, we set about building an MVP. In this case, we created a payment processing product using physical card terminals as the first step before starting to build the app. The idea was that once we established Pulsare Pay, we could then add new features and integrate with existing providers like Visa, Mastercard and Coinbase. The beauty of the staggered roll-out was that we would start getting feedback from customers, have a platform to expand upon and would begin to generate some all-important revenue almost straight away.

We could have waited until we got the complete package ready to launch with all the various options available. That might have taken months, even years, to get just right and, even then, there would have been no guarantee of success. It's much better to go live and start exposing your idea to the real-world problems you'll inevitably find, and build the business from there.

Early validation

When you're building a start-up, the goal isn't to make your product or service perfect, it's to get it working. An MVP is the minimum version of your product that proves your idea works. You're not building the dream yet, you're building the test.

An MVP is about a lot more than getting a product out quickly so you can start making some cash, although that's always nice. It's about validating your idea by putting it in front of real customers – genuine feedback beats educated guesses every time. Even if you're passionate about your concept and your market research suggests there's demand, there's no substitute for actual user reactions. You don't know what works until people engage with it.

Testing on a small scale by releasing a stripped-down, functional version of your concept or product will give you insights into what about it customers value, what confuses them and what they'll ignore altogether. This will allow you to focus on what truly matters and not waste resources on building features or infrastructure that may never be used. A full-scale launch based on flawed assumptions will be an expensive and irreversible mistake. Testing your product on a small scale allows you to fail safely and cheaply, learning critical lessons without overcommitting your money and time.

An MVP is also a handy testbed for refining your product before going out to a wider customer base. It will show you what breaks, where the bottlenecks are and which parts of your system aren't ready for selling at volume. It's like shaking a machine to see which bolts come loose. Once you can see all the pain points, you can test alternative designs. The iterative cycle makes the final product not only more polished but also more in line with customer expectations (and always be honest with them that the MVP is a work in progress). Since they are the ones who will be paying for it, all being well, this increases your chances of achieving product–market fit – or, in other words, success.

Alternative MVPs

Not all products are the same. Sometimes it's just not feasible to build a 'minimum' version, especially when you're dealing with physical goods. If your idea involves expensive tooling, custom manufacturing or complex logistics, then the instruction to just 'build a prototype' is a lot easier said than done.

If this is the case with the product you have in mind, then you need to separate testing the idea from building it. Forget about finding a factory and investing thousands to see if your prospective customers want what you're making. Instead, your MVP can be a simple website, a landing page that describes the product as if it already exists, alongside a 'Buy Now' button. You could take this one step further, if budget allows, by making a working, stripped-down prototype using a 3D printer and demoing it in a video. In either case, when someone clicks through the 'Buy Now' button, instead of taking their money, thank them for their interest and put them on a waiting list. You'll validate demand without needing to produce a single finished item. The next step is to get in touch with the potential customer to find out exactly what interested them in your product and what they are hoping to get out of it. This kind of lightweight testing works surprisingly well for physical products. It helps you gauge interest, test pricing and refine your pitch, without having to spend a penny on production.

Digital MVPs

With tech products, you can go much further. Thanks to cloud infrastructure, open-source frameworks and no-code tools, it's never been easier to build a basic version of a digital product that's enough to check for potential demand and stress-test features. Restraint is critical here. Just because you *can* build all the features, doesn't mean you should. The key is knowing what to include and what to leave out.

All products will be different but, as a rule of thumb, figuring out what your digital MVP should look like comes down to understanding what your product needs to have or do to prove its value. You want the bare minimum to test your assumptions. Nothing more. Then, once your product is launched, you can move on to things that will improve the experience.

With Pulsare Pay, there were certain features that absolutely had to be there from the start. For example, users had to be able to take money using the physical card terminal. Without that, the entire experience fell apart. When it came to wider features, such as customer admin panels, for example, where the user could track their customer interactions over time, well, that could wait.

Here are some examples of what might be considered basic essential elements for a digital MVP, and things that could be later improvements or additions.

THE HUSTLE MINDSET

Digital MVPs – the essentials

Build now	Build later
Core problem-solving feature: Single function that solves the user's main pain point	Advanced features: Anything not critical to solving the core problem
Basic UX: Clean, functional interface to enable use	Polished visual design: Branding, custom graphics and animations
User onboarding (minimal): Simple explanation or tutorial, can be a landing page or App shell	In-depth walkthroughs or tutorials: Develop these in line with additional functionality
Working sign-up/login: To capture users and measure interest	Multi-factor authentication
A single feedback mechanism: Basic way to collect user feedback, could be a form, or an email link	Integrated support chat, AI helpdesk
'Buy Now'/'Sign Up' button: Triggers action, even if it only leads to a waiting list	Payment integration, shopping cart
Data tracking (basic analytics): See what people use or ignore	Complex dashboards and custom metric platforms
Manual or semi-automated backend: Humans can simulate features behind the scenes	Full automation, custom admin panels
Device/platform compatibility: Primary target only, eg mobile or web	Cross-platform compatibility, native apps
Bug-free for core use: It will be basic, but make sure it works	Total stability across the whole platform

With a digital MVP, the product should function, but don't overbuild it. At this stage, there is no requirement for dashboards, AI integration or three levels of onboarding. You need the one core feature that will prove whether people care enough to use it, pay for it or recommend it. Find the easiest (and cheapest) way to make it useable so that people can get started without a manual, then have a way for them to give feedback.

Don't get distracted by fancy extras. If your users can't access the main thing your product promises, or just aren't interested in it, the rest doesn't matter.

Using tech to build and validate your MVP

If you're serious about testing your concept quickly and efficiently, you need to leverage every tool available. There are countless systems out there that perform incredible tasks at a fraction of the cost of traditional testing models and new ones are appearing all the time.

In Chapter 4, I stressed the importance of data and target marketing. With AI, you can sift through mountains of data in minutes, spot trends and fine-tune your idea at a pace that would previously have taken months. It's like having a research team working for you around the clock, turning raw data into actionable insights. AI also lets you validate your concept in weeks instead of months, whether you're analysing market trends, refining your marketing strategy or optimising operations.

These are the tools I would look at, along with an idea of how they might help you.

No-code product builders to build your digital MVP fast

Tool	Use case	How it helps with MVP validation
Bubble	Visual web app builder	Helps you create full-featured, database-driven MVPs without code. Build user dashboards, sign-up flows and logic for early testing.
Webflow	Website builder with CMS	Ideal for landing pages, or lightweight marketing sites. Use it to explain your product, showcase benefits and collect email sign-ups.
Carrd	Ultra-fast landing page	Build a simple 'one-page' site to pitch your MVP and collect emails.

Forms and surveys to capture interest and feedback

Tool	Use case	How it helps with MVP validation
Tally	Simple, elegant forms	Use for waiting lists, pricing preference testing, feature voting or pre-order interest.

Typeform	Conversational surveys	Create user-friendly, engaging feedback forms or quizzes to test customer understanding or gauge interest.
Google Forms	Basic form builder	Good for free, no-frills surveys during initial testing phases.

Analytics and behaviour tracking to identify and measure what works

Tool	Use case	How it helps with MVP validation
Mixpanel	Event-based product analytics	Track specific user actions like sign-ups, feature use and customer dropouts.
Hotjar	Heatmaps and user recordings	See exactly how users interact with your MVP: where they click, scroll, get stuck or leave.
PostHog	Open-source analytics with session recording	Ideal for private or self-hosted MVPs, combines product analytics with recordings and feature flags.

THE HUSTLE MINDSET

Automation tools to simulate functionality and save time

Tool	Use case	How it helps with MVP validation
Zapier	App automation	Connect apps, eg form–email–CRM, without code. Good for simulating backend features.
Make	Complex workflow automation	Like Zapier, but with deeper logic and branching. Useful for simulating multi-step workflows in an MVP.

General AI tools to create, build and learn more quickly

Tool	Use case	How it helps with MVP validation
ChatGPT	AI assistant helps with ideas, content and code	Write landing page copy, generate form questions and FAQs, summarise feedback or simulate a customer support chatbot for your MVP.
Copy.ai/Jasper	AI writing tools	Create landing page or emails to test messaging.
Claude	Research	Validate assumptions with AI-powered summaries and competitor research.

Extras including nice-to-have tools for validation

Tool	Use case	How it helps with MVP validation
Calendly	Schedule calls with early users	Book one-to-one feedback with potential customers.
Loom	Video walkthroughs	Record a quick walkthrough to explain more complex products, or explain key features.
Outseta	All-in-one start-up backend	Combine login, CRM, billing and email tools. Great for lean MVPs.
Notion	Internal project management or documentation	Use as a public roadmap or early knowledge base for testers.

As well as the above, I'd also recommend you do your own research, in case something more effective appears. Bear in mind that, to get the most out of it, you need to understand AI prompting; I would highly recommend doing a short course to gauge the basics so you can use AI to its full advantage.

The above list might seem a little daunting, because it highlights all the elements that go into creating a single MVP. You can relax, though. You don't need an expensive development team to test ideas. You just need to know how to combine the right tools.

Once again, my advice is to break it down into bite-sized pieces. A typical MVP flow using the tools above might look like this:

1. **Build landing page:** Webflow or Carrd
2. **Capture email:** Tally and Zapier, into Notion/Google Sheet
3. **Track clicks:** Mixpanel or Hotjar
4. **Send automated emails:** Zapier or Outseta
5. **Collect feedback:** Typeform survey
6. **Refine based on usage:** Hotjar recordings and Mixpanel funnel

Using tools like this will accelerate your progress while giving you a clear, data-backed view of what's working and what's not. It's faster, smarter and significantly less risky than building in the dark. It's not nearly as daunting as it sounds either, even if you don't consider yourself tech minded; the tools are accessible, intuitive and incredibly powerful.

Finding testers and collecting feedback

Who, then, are going to be your first testers? You want brave, early adopters who'll ask sensible questions, and give you honest feedback on what is working and what isn't. Most people go for the obvious choice of family and friends. A word of warning, though: it's crucial that early testers are completely honest. People close to you may just say what they think you want to hear because they know how much it means to you; or they may be really bloody-minded, telling you it's a rubbish idea just to wind you up.

Your first users should be people with a real need for the product you've come up with, not just a passing curiosity. They're likely to be more forgiving, more honest and more engaged, because what you're building solves a pain point for them. Often, they're already looking for a solution like yours. Equally, they can be brutally honest if the product doesn't solve the problem, but they will also tell you why, so you can adjust as necessary. All you need to do is to find where they're already hanging out.

To do this, go online. There is a strong chance that there's a niche subreddit, Slack community or LinkedIn group where a bunch of people are complaining about the problem you're trying to solve. There are online communities for every grumble imaginable these days; some of them may even be in your own network, and perhaps is what gave you your idea in the first place. For Pulsare Pay, we tapped into our networks. We knew a lot of small business owners and brought them in early to get their honest thoughts.

Share your MVP directly online with whichever group/s is/are relevant to your new business and ask them what they think. Alternatively, if you are launching a physical product and have some prototypes ready, you could consider a local pop-up or market stall to test your product face to face.

One of the big decisions to make at this stage is: do you charge for your MVP, or offer it for free in exchange for feedback? Ultimately, this comes down to the value of the item. If your product solves a real business problem, especially in B2B, you should charge from day one, even if it's just a small amount. If people won't pay for the MVP, they won't pay for the full version either. Alternatively, you can offer the MVP as a free sample but tell customers they will need to pay for the full version when it is ready. You can offer early users free access and priority onboarding because you need feedback, but make it clear that it won't stay free so that they feel they are getting something of real value. That way, they'll take it seriously from the off.

Feedback is what you are doing this for, so make it as easy as possible for testers to give you their views. Where possible, I like to arrange local tester meetups or networking events. Apart from getting your name out there, it is much better to hear feedback first-hand because the best analysis often comes through casual conversations. To get started, ask a few open-ended questions and then just listen. People will tell you what's confusing about your product/service, what's missing and what they wish it did. Listen out for gold dust statements like:

- 'I can't figure out how to do X.'
- 'Is there a way to do Y?'
- 'It's not clear what happens when I press this.'

Once you've had clear pointers like this, you can ask further questions and really dig into what works and what doesn't. For example, when we tested Pulsare Pay, we got a lot of questions around trust. People wanted to know how payments were handled and whether their data was secure.

Again, use a mix of technology to collect, compile and process as much feedback data as you can. Try a combination of:

- One-on-one conversations (DMs, calls, Zoom meetings)
- Screen recordings and heatmaps (via tools like Hotjar)
- Simple feedback forms (Google Forms, Typeform)
- Watching how people use the platform

This step is not about getting thousands of users on day one. It's about getting the *right kind* of users, those close enough to the issue to give genuinely useful feedback.

Once you have that feedback, don't waste it. Organise all criticism into three categories:

1. **Urgent fixes** – things that ruin the experience
2. **Priority improvements** – changes that would boost value
3. **Non-essentials** – ideas worth noting, but not to be dealt with now

When you have a list of concerns that fall into each category, prioritise category one and stay focused on fixing what's stopping users from getting value today. You can work down the lists to get to the non-essentials in category three later.

Negative feedback

Be prepared for the response to your MVP to be underwhelming. The feedback might be blunt, along the lines of, 'I don't need this,' or, 'This is rubbish.' Or, worse still, silence. It's tough, but it is a positive. Look at it this way: if no one wants your MVP, no one is going to want the all-singing, all-dancing polished version that you will have spent tens of thousands on either. If this is the case, it's not failure – it is priceless information.

Across the board negative feedback is the most underrated source of competitive advantage there is. I say 'across the board' because there will always be naysayers, people who say, 'Nah, it's rubbish,' just to make a point. What I am talking about here is widespread, consistent feedback that the idea is not a goer. It's a good thing if you hear the resounding message that 'this doesn't solve my problem' when you've only built a scrappy prototype. You can then go back, refine it and come up with an idea that does hit the mark.

Move forward, pivot or start again?

Depending on how negative the feedback is, you need to decide whether to pivot or junk the original idea and start again completely. To be clear, a pivot is a strategic shift where you keep the original vision of solving a particular problem but change one or more core elements of the product. This might mean targeting a different type of customer, or making what you thought was a secondary feature the star of the show. Starting again, on the other hand, means abandoning the idea completely and finding a new solution for a new audience.

Whether you choose to pivot or start again will be based on your own interpretation of the feedback you've received from the testers. As a guide, though, if users were not engaged at all, signing up but never returning or abandoned the MVP quickly, this suggests that it is not hitting the mark and it's time to start over. However, if they gravitate towards an unexpected aspect of the solution, then you've solved the problem but in a different way than you first imagined. It's possible that pivoting towards that feature as the solution is the right call.

One caveat here: don't be too quick to pivot before testing your assumptions, or you could find yourself bouncing around trying to please everyone but not pleasing anyone at all. Meanwhile, you'll be wasting a ton of money and even more of your time. If you can, check in with your testers to see if they find the new version you are proposing more compelling. One-on-one interviews are a great way to really dig into what gets people excited – and what doesn't. Then, if a pivot does look like the best way forward, build a new MVP and repeat the tests you did for the first version to make sure you are on track.

At some point you will need to make the call to move beyond the MVP and into building and launching the product. The right time for this is a decision only you can make, but there are a few clear clues you are onto a good thing:

- Users stop reporting bugs and start asking for features
- You get unsolicited positive feedback
- People start recommending your product to others
- Revenue starts to come in consistently

When this happens, it is time to go live.

6
Partnerships

Pick up any book on business and it'll tell you that partnerships are the way forward if you want your business to succeed. The logic seems solid: two heads are better than one and a good partner can cover your weaknesses. It sounds great – in theory. In reality? A bad partnership can kill a business before it even has a chance to get off the ground, let alone succeed. If you don't go into a partnership with your eyes wide open, you're setting yourself up for a world of pain. I mean this – it's horrendous when a partnership goes bad.

Do you *need* a partner? Not necessarily. At least, not right at the beginning. When you are starting a business, it can sometimes be better to go it alone, especially when things are messy and you're still figuring stuff out. There is a point, though, where having a partner can be a huge asset. Not just someone to split the work with, but someone to challenge you, fill in the gaps and push the business forward.

One of the biggest shifts you'll experience when you decide to start your own business is that the social environment around you changes. Or perhaps a better way to put it is that your *perception* of your environment changes. If all your friends work nine-to-five jobs and have no interest in business or entrepreneurialism, you're going to struggle to find common ground with them. They won't have any idea what you are trying to do and have even less enthusiasm for it. People are inherently self-centred, and will quickly switch off when a friend keeps rambling about their 'world-beating' business idea. The problem here is that it can be quite difficult to motivate yourself if you have no one to speak to about what you're trying to do. It's helpful to surround yourself with like-minded people to bounce ideas off and get feedback from. Just by having the right conversations with the right people, new ideas will come more naturally and develop more quickly. This is a significant reason for finding a business partner. They will be a person working alongside you, who is just as interested in the business and completely invested in its success. They'll want to talk about it all the time too.

Starting a business is an intense experience, with endless decisions to make, constant firefighting and uncertainty. A partner, or co-founder, can share the emotional and operational burden, meaning you are less likely to become overwhelmed, make unwise knee-jerk decisions or, let's face it, collapse with exhaustion because you are trying to do everything alone. A good business partner will help you move faster and think sharper, but a bad one will drain your energy and slow you down.

Qualities to look for

Business partnerships are like marriages. If you don't have the hard conversations and ask the tough questions upfront, you'll be dealing with the fallout later. It's easy to get caught up in the excitement of starting something new and make all sorts of assumptions in the heat of the moment. Since I've had the benefit of getting it wrong a few times, I've learned some things along the way. Now, I make sure to take my time choosing business partners, and every partnership agreement is watertight. This is not because I expect things to go wrong, but because I know that setting clear expectations from day one will save me a world of trouble down the line if they do.

A badly thought through partnership can take everything you've built and burn it to the ground. The lesson? Take your time, follow the advice in this chapter and think carefully about who you choose to work with. There are three qualities that I prioritise when looking for a partner:

1. Trust
2. Complementary skills
3. Energy

Trust

Trust is number one for me. If I have to question a partner's intentions, it's a no-go. I've got to trust that when things hit the fan, they'll still show up.

You can't oversee everything in a start-up, and things move quickly. You've got to feel sure that your partner is going to act in the business' best interest, even if you are not looking over their shoulder. Don't forget, businesses live or die by the speed with which you react. If you are stalling or losing pace because you are continually second-guessing your partner, or duplicating effort by double checking their work, you'll lose momentum and time.

The need for absolute trust is why I take my time choosing a partner. You need to see what people are like under pressure, when clients are difficult or something goes wrong. Poppy, who I mentioned earlier, worked alongside me in our businesses for four years before I approached her about partnering with me in one of my newest business ventures.

I hadn't hired Poppy in the traditional sense. We'd originally worked together at another company and when I went off to build something new, she came with me. At that point, she was technically an employee, but I never saw her as 'just' staff. From early on, there was something about the way she carried herself. She just got it. She understood what needed to be done and did it without being asked. She picked things up fast, and always showed up with the right energy.

PARTNERSHIPS

She wasn't the loudest in the room, but she was the most consistent. The truth is, I didn't realise what I had at the time. We worked alongside each other for years, building, growing, grinding, and it wasn't until later that I stepped back and really saw her for what she was: the perfect business partner, right under my nose.

Over the years of working together, we'd built something rare: real trust. I've had business partners before, some were friends, others sold me a dream, but more often than not, those situations ended in disappointment. Promises weren't kept, values didn't align and under pressure cracks were always revealed. With Poppy, it was different. There was no big pitch, no sales talk, just a steady, reliable support day in and day out. She didn't need to sell me a vision; she lived it alongside me. The relationship evolved naturally and now she's not just someone I work with; she's someone I trust with the future of everything we've built.

Partnering with someone you've worked with beforehand might not be a possibility for you, particularly if you are starting your first venture. But there are still things you can try to emulate from this experience. Start small. Do a project together. Build something. See how they operate under pressure. Anyone can show up for a coffee and a chat with good energy, what matters is how they act when shit's not going to plan. You'll learn fast if they're going to be an asset or are just playing business.

Complementary skills

At this point, you might be thinking, 'Great! I'll bring in my best mate Dave; I trust him and we've known each other for years.' Don't do it. First, he may be a great person to have a pint with and will always bring you your change if you ask him to get something from the shop, but is he battle-tested in business? Second, 'getting on well' with someone is not enough. As well as trust, there's a second quality that needs to be fulfilled in a business partner: complementary skills. A good relationship is no guarantee of this; in fact, if you are friends, there's a strong chance you'll be quite similar.

It is tempting to partner with someone who thinks like you, talks like you and gets excited by the same things. It feels safe and comfortable. But building a founding team of 'mini-mes' is one of the fastest ways to hit a ceiling. You end up doubling down on strengths and leaving your blind spots wide open. I want someone who thinks differently and sees things I don't, but who wants the same end result. A business needs range: vision and execution; creativity and structure; sales and systems.

Choosing a partner with complementary skills, not overlapping ones, gives your start-up more balance, better coverage and a stronger foundation. If you're super creative, find someone who thrives on technical detail. If you're great with ideas but hate spreadsheets, look for someone who can model the business. That contrast will occasionally create tension, yes, but the right kind of tension – the kind that leads to sharper decisions, better problem solving and healthier debate.

Of course, seeking out complementary skills means identifying your weaknesses. It is not easy to admit what you are not good at. The best approach is to begin by working out what it is that you do well and then move on to what skills you might need to shore up and any areas where you could do a bit better. Set aside some time to list ten of your strongest skills. Are you, for example, a strategic thinker, or great at sales, or brilliant with the numbers? Then, list the skills you are lacking and where you might need a little help.

Once you have your list, use it to assess possible partners against and do a version for them. If the person you have in mind has a similar set of skills to you, it might be best to think again. If their skills are mostly ones you don't have, this could be a strong, productive partnership. You can then focus on building a collaboration where you each have your own lane and trust each other to handle the things that fall into it. As the business evolves, roles will inevitably shift and that's fine too. You've got to be flexible.

Energy

One of those things I have learned about myself over the years is I've got very high standards, not just for others, but for myself. I don't like half measures or people who coast. This is doubly, even triply so when it comes to partners. I want to work with people who finish.

Talk is cheap, but progress isn't. Start-ups live or die by execution. Ideas alone don't validate markets, acquire users, raise investment or build products. There are too many talkers in business. I want doers. A 'doer' is someone who gets things moving, builds momentum and doesn't wait for perfect conditions to act. Doers don't just plan, they make things happen. When resources are limited and there's no one else to delegate to, a doer will roll up their sleeves and figure it out. That might mean designing the landing page, cold-emailing a hundred potential customers, building a no-code prototype or chasing overdue invoices. In a high-uncertainty environment, progress beats polish.

Just as importantly, a doer keeps energy and morale high among everyone else. Inaction is contagious, but so is action. When one founder is visibly getting things done, it creates a ripple effect across the team. It sets a standard and builds belief. It'll have a great impact on you, too. I know that working with the right people has made me sharper, more self-aware and more focused. You learn quickly what kind of energy builds momentum and what slows it down.

Setting expectations

A client, James, is a hugely successful business founder, but he's not a natural frontman. He's smart, measured and brilliant with numbers, but quiet, perhaps even a bit socially awkward. He knew he needed someone to drive sales, so he hired a seasoned salesperson with a strong CV and a big personality. Part of the package was that this person became a partner in James's firm. At first, it seemed like the perfect fit and a win–win for them both. The sales guy hit the ground running, brought in a bunch of deals, and said all the right things in meetings with James, talking about growing the business and taking it to the next level. But slowly, the dynamics began to shift.

The salesperson started to take over more than just sales and began to steer the culture. He became the loudest voice in the room, making suggestions about who to hire and fire and changing processes that had been in place long before he had arrived. Ultimately, he was acting like the business was his. James, unsure how to confront the imbalance, let it slide for a bit. The longer he let it go on though, the more this guy muscled in on areas that were nothing to do with him. Eventually, it went too far and James had to intervene. By then, though, it was inevitable that what came next would be messy, emotional and disruptive. James struggled to rein him back in without this derailing the business, and it almost did.

The lesson here is that James should have set clear boundaries and expectations before he presented a partnership agreement. For once, he had deviated from his thoughtful, considered approach, no doubt in his enthusiasm to sign up a salesperson who he hoped would transform the company fortunes. As it turned out, the salesperson did transform the business, but not in the way James envisaged.

It's always an exciting moment when you find someone who seems to be the ideal partner, and there's a temptation to just get on with it and deal with the 'boring bits' later. If you think setting out exactly who does what falls into this category, you're making a big mistake. Don't wait until things go wrong to start thinking about contracts, agreements and setting out clear roles. Lay it all out from day one. Who does what? How do decisions get made? What happens if someone wants out? These conversations might feel awkward at the start, but trust me, they're a lot easier than dealing with the mess of a broken business later. You don't need to overcomplicate it, but you do need to get aligned, otherwise you could be on two different paths and not realise it until it's too late.

As a bare minimum, get an agreement on the financials, communication between partners, how you'll take big decisions and what will happen if you sell, or one of you wants out. These are the key points of a partnership, so we'll talk about each of these in turn.

Finances

I often say that the financial side is the elephant in the room when you are setting up a business partnership. You'll meet a potential partner and talk about the goals of the business and who will do what, and all they really want to know before they commit is what

PARTNERSHIPS

they will get out of it. That's fair enough. Why would anyone sign up to all the effort that comes with a start-up without knowing how much they stand to make?

As a matter of course, I get this conversation out of the way early on. That way, they'll know if they are interested and will be able to properly focus on the rest. To clarify, I don't spring this on them during the first conversation. The early chats are informal discussions to see if we get along. But when you have the first formal meeting to discuss a possible partnership, you need to cover this point.

Below is a list of financial considerations I would want to agree on in this meeting, covering investment expectations, ownership and equity and plans for future funding. Use this as a checklist in your partnership discussions:

1. How much is each person contributing (cash, time, assets)?
2. Will the contributions be equal or varied?
3. Is the funding staged, or up front?
4. What happens if someone can't meet their commitments?
5. Are equity shares based on contribution, role or future milestones?
6. What happens if someone exits early?
7. Will you seek external funding? If so, when?

8. Are you aligned on valuation and dilution expectations?

9. Who will lead fundraising conversations?

While you are on the subject of money, talk about who will handle the day-to-day financial decisions in the running of the business. Do major expenses need to be agreed by both partners? Who will have authority to authorise payments and to what limit? Transparency is key when it comes to finances. I don't care who's managing the numbers – everyone needs visibility. Use shared accounts, track the money and review regularly. If the money side isn't clean, this will always lead to problems. Decide early who handles what, but make sure no one has unchecked control.

Communication

This is especially important in these days of hybrid working. How often are you going to talk to one another if you are not in the same place, and how? I'd say you should check in with a partner at least once a day, if not more, especially in the pre-launch phase. If you have an upfront agreement on this, it can be a helpful red flag when things start to drift. In one of my businesses, there are four main partners who are based all over the place. We aim to Zoom first thing every morning; this is an important exercise where we tell each other what we've been doing and hold each other accountable. If a partner missed one or two of these calls, it would be a concern. Reliable and consistent communication is a sign of professionalism and commitment, and makes sure you spot potential issues early.

Don't only make plans to talk about what is happening in the here and now, and all the fires you are fighting. Set up a regular meeting to talk about the direction of the business at least once a month, minimum. Weekly is better. You've got to make time to zoom out and talk about what's working, what's not and where you're headed. Otherwise, you just end up running in circles without realising you're off track.

Taking big decisions

When it comes to taking big decisions, I'm not precious about being right. I only care about making the best move for the business. I want to find the best way to lay it all on the table and hash it out with my business partners. Sometimes we will debate an issue and sometimes one of us will defer to the other's experience. But the agreement you need to come to is that once you decide on a course of action, you are all in.

Exit plans

It might feel awkward and uncomfortable discussing what happens if one of you wants to leave the business, but it is better to discuss it when everyone is feeling good about what comes next. People change, they have kids, want to move away, they burn out or pivot their career aspirations. That's life. Plan for it while things are still good, not when emotions are running high.

Talk about what leaving looks like, how equity is handled and how responsibilities will be passed on. If you've got that covered early, it's easier to stay focused on the here and now.

Don't get caught up in selling the dream and avoid the difficult chats, assuming any hiccups between you will work themselves out. They won't. If someone is going to be involved in your business in a meaningful way, you need to have the hard conversations now, before emotions, egos and money get in the way.

Due diligence

I've been doing this for a long while, so I like to think I am a much better judge of character than I was at the beginning. But I still make mistakes. We all do. That is why, when you think you have found your ideal partner, you need to take a beat and do some checks before committing. A lawyer once put this bit to me really well. He said something along the lines of, 'It all starts swimmingly, and you are skipping along hand-in-hand, happily chatting about all the amazing things you are going to achieve together, and then, when the going gets tough, the cracks will start to show.'

All being well, you won't need to resort to enforcing contracts when the going gets tough. After all, as entrepreneurs, that is what you're signing up for. But if you've never done it before, it is impossible to say how you or your partner will react under pressure. Some people just can't hack the work involved in setting up and running a new business. The worst-case scenario is when one partner can handle it and the other can't, and the one who can ends up doing everything, while the one who can't sits on their backside. I've had that happen to me a few times. It will drive you mad if you find yourself in that situation.

When you are still at the 'getting to know you' stage, do some background checks. You wouldn't hire an employee without checking their references, so why would you go blindly into business with someone as important as a partner? Tell them what you're doing and, most likely, they'll willingly help you with the process. Don't forget online sources either – Google or ChatGPT might have something to add. Offer them the same courtesy and put them in touch with some of your own referees. If you have mutual acquaintances, ask them what they think. Find out about your potential partner's reputation. You're not being paranoid; you're protecting your time and the business.

Contracts

If the background checks come back good, it is time to make things official with a contract to make it a formal partnership. If funds are available, I would always invest in using a good start-up lawyer. They'll flag stuff you've never even thought about and it will save you a lot of potential headaches later. If you are light on cash, this is not an excuse to skip this step altogether – there are lots of free partnership agreements available online, and you can use ChatGPT. But I really would recommend investing in legal advice if you possibly can, you won't regret it.

At the bare minimum, the contract between the partners should cover:

1. **Business details:**

    - Name of the partnership

    - Business purpose and activities

    - Registered address

2. **Capital contributions:**

    - How much each partner is investing (money, assets, time)

    - Whether contributions are equal or different

    - Terms for future contributions or capital calls

3. **Ownership and profit sharing:**

    - Ownership percentages

    - How profits and losses will be split

    - Whether partners draw salaries or take profit shares

4. **Roles and responsibilities:**
    - Who is responsible for what (day-to-day roles, key decisions, legal duties)
    - Decision-making structure (unanimous or majority vote for certain issues)
    - Who manages bank accounts and finances

5. **Intellectual property:**
    - Who owns what IP
    - What happens to IP if a partner leaves
    - How new IP created in the business is handled

6. **Dispute resolution:**
    - How disagreements will be handled (eg mediation, arbitration)
    - A process to resolve deadlocks
    - Decision authority in a tie

7. **Exit, death or retirement:**
    - What happens if a partner wants to leave
    - Buyout clauses and valuation process
    - What happens in the event of death or incapacity

8. **Non-compete and confidentiality:**
    - Restrictions on starting or working for competing businesses

- Protection of trade secrets and sensitive information

9. **Dissolution:**

    - Terms for ending the partnership
    - How assets, liabilities and responsibilities will be divided

10. **Legal and governing terms:**

    - Which law governs the agreement (usually UK law)
    - Review clause (eg reviewed annually or upon a major change)

A partnership agreement is non-negotiable. If you're serious, put it on paper. It doesn't matter how good the vibes are now, people change and business gets messy.

When things go wrong

Like nearly everything I'm sharing here, I learned the hard way how to deal with partnerships that go wrong. This is another cautionary tale from one of my early businesses, when I went into partnership with Matt to set up a training company.

I knew Matt from working with him in one of my paid jobs and he seemed like a nice enough bloke. Like all businesses, there was a lot of graft involved in getting the training company off the ground. We were building it from an 'office' at my mum's place for about four to five months. At the start, we had a couple of small clients but couldn't afford to pay ourselves, so I had to take on a job as a Tesco delivery driver just to cover my bills while we got things going. I say 'my bills' but I was basically funding both of us at that point. After around three months, we were bringing in just enough that I could quit Tesco and focus on the business full time.

Once we got our first bit of investment, things started to shift, especially with Matt. We got an office, hired staff and had some money behind us, but suddenly he started going off the radar. He would miss meetings and show up late every day. Then, he kept disappearing for doctor's appointments, up to three or four of them a week. When I asked him if he was alright, he batted away my questions. Something wasn't adding up and he wasn't pulling his weight. What made it even more frustrating was that he was posting all over Instagram about his life as a super-successful entrepreneur.

The final straw was when the company credit card vanished. I asked if he had it and he said no, but the next week, transactions popped up all over the area where he lived. After a bit more digging around, I found that all the 'doctor's appointments' were complete fiction. At that point, the trust was gone. He was lying, not showing up and putting me in a bad spot financially, plus I'd been working flat-out to keep things going while he was playing games.

I was pretty upset about it all and the way I handled it wasn't ideal – I confronted him and we ended up in a full-on argument. When we'd calmed down a bit, Matt admitted that he was having problems with his girlfriend and said that he felt bad about lying to me. After a bit more discussion, we agreed he'd leave the company and sign his shares over to me.

That experience taught me a lot about people. Loyalty at the start doesn't mean someone's got what it takes for the long haul. And if they show you that they can't be trusted, believe them the first time.

I'd handle that situation differently now and lead with the facts, not the emotions – though that can be tough when you put your heart and soul into a business. If I could go back, I'd have made sure the meeting stayed calm and respectful, having taken time to reflect before going in all guns blazing. Most of all, I wish I had said something right at the beginning, when Matt had first started showing signs of being distracted and not showing up.

If things start going wrong, the difficult conversation needs to be had right away. Talk it out, even if it is uncomfortable, because when you let things build up in silence, it destroys the trust that is so vital to a good partnership. All being well, an honest and thorough conversation early on, where you both agree on a way forward, gives you a very good chance of getting things back on track. If all else fails, provided you have a partnership agreement, you will both be protected.

7
Building A Team Of Believers

In the last chapter, I told the story of my failed partnership and how that resolved. But while the story ended for Matt when he left the training company, for me it continued. I was suddenly left to carry everything on my own. That's when I learned one of the hardest lessons in business: hiring and managing a team is a completely different ballgame from selling a product or service. When you're starting out, it's easy to assume that getting people on board will transform everything for the better. In reality, it can make or break everything.

In this chapter, I'll talk about hiring; I'll then go into how to manage your new team in the next.

Recruitment

I've made every hiring mistake in the book. I've rushed the process, interviewed a handful of people and picked the best of the bunch, assuming it would work out. It usually didn't and I've had to unravel bad hires more times than I can count, wasting time and energy trying to fix the damage. What I didn't understand then is that recruitment is a numbers game. You can't just see three people and hope for the best. Successful hiring requires volume. You need to see eight, ten, even fifteen candidates to find the right one. You're not just looking for the right mix of know-how, skills and qualifications either. You need so much more than that. The best people aren't just talented, they actually believe in what you're trying to build.

And it's not just about what you're looking for in them – you also need them to be looking at *you*. The other side to this challenge is finding people who are prepared to take the risk of joining a start-up. After all, you've got no big brand name, no cushy salaries and no job security to offer. You need to find people who aren't just looking for a pay cheque. They have to see the vision, buy into it and want to be part of the journey. This means you need to be crystal clear on what you're building and why. If you're not passionate or excited about the business, how can you expect anyone else to be?

BUILDING A TEAM OF BELIEVERS

How to recruit well is not a lesson I learned overnight. It took a long time and a lot of mistakes. I don't get it right 100% of the time even now, but I am a lot better at it. Probably because I have interviewed hundreds of people, and practice really does make perfect – or at least makes a big difference. I think about it this way: if you're a footballer, you have to go training three, four or five times a week, and play in lots of matches. If you just sat at home and only played on a Sunday, you'd probably be the worst player in the team. It is the same with interviewing for new recruits. Once you've interviewed multiple people and then worked with them, got it right and wrong, seen the genuine people and the not so genuine, you start to get an idea of what people are about. You can't put a price on that sort of experience, and it's not something you can get from a training course. It's about tuning your antennae through seeing lots of candidates, and making sure you have done an exhaustive search. Today, I can sit in a room with someone and I'll probably know within the first twenty seconds if I'll give them a chance or not. It's not about being judgemental, it's about picking up the subtle cues that indicate whether someone aligns with our company culture and values. I couldn't always do that.

Of course, in the beginning, you won't have the benefit of all that practice. Until you build up experience, you'll need to rely heavily on instinct, though I can fast track you through the learning process by telling you what to look out for.

An over-the-top hiring process

There is no cutting corners when it comes to recruiting a great team. Hiring is crucial, not a side task. This was another lesson that I learned the hard way when I tried hiring a member of my own family for a role. This had to be a good idea, right? They were flesh and blood, so of course I could trust them. Wrong and wrong.

One of my early ventures was a gym that I had acquired at a great price. I brought a family member in as a manager. He was a fitness enthusiast who went to the gym a lot and I assumed he had some of the same entrepreneurial genes as me since we knew each other well. Initially, it did go smoothly. I invested in equipment and in renovating the space, and was soon trusting the manager to handle daily operations while I attended to my other businesses. However, problems surfaced quickly. What I didn't immediately realise was that he was consistently disappearing early, leaving the gym without any management oversight. The rest of the staff cottoned onto this pretty fast and were soon mirroring his lax attitude. It wasn't just poor timekeeping, either. Thanks to his less-than-inspirational leadership, standards across the board slipped. Inevitably, customers noticed and the complaints started to roll in.

After some uncomfortable conversations, I had to remove him from the role and recruit a successor in a hurry, hoping the replacement would save the business. But hiring shouldn't be rushed and, unfortunately, the new manager wasn't any better, compounding the problems with an already shaky business. Staff morale continued to decline, cash handling became problematic and we even discovered theft by employees. Eventually, we cut our losses and sold the gym at a significant financial loss.

What did this all teach me? Well, as outlined earlier in the book, family and friends are not always the trusted resource they might seem to be. There are no guarantees that they will be great hires, and you may be less rigorous in the hiring process than you would with an unknown. Plus, there is the emotional fallout if it doesn't work out. If you have to fire a family member, I can guarantee that Christmas and birthday gatherings will be very awkward for a good while afterwards.

You need to start from scratch and be extremely rigorous in your hiring process. I would go as far as to say you need to be over the top in how thorough you are. It doesn't matter if you don't think the position is particularly important or senior enough to spend much time on. Every position in a start-up is crucial, and you need to be super selective.

Going 'over the top' means making time for multi-step interviews, trial tasks and team introductions. If all that sounds like a lot of hard work, remind yourself that being extra picky initially is a hundred times easier than undoing a bad hire. One wrong person in a start-up can derail momentum, drain your time and damage team culture. Being over the top means being thorough, relentless and unapologetically selective in order to protect your company's future.

In the table below, I set out the bare minimum for a rigorous start-up hiring process:

Hiring process

Clear role definition	Write a job spec that's not just about tasks, but mindset. Spell out what kind of person thrives in your culture.
Pre-screening application questions	Add a couple of written questions to your job post. For example: • What excites you about start-ups? • Describe a time you solved a problem independently. This filters out people who don't care or can't communicate clearly.
Phone screen (10-15 mins)	A quick vibe check: Are they sharp? Curious? Do they understand the role? If it feels off, don't move forward.
Zoom, Teams or Google Meet interview (30-45 mins)	This is where you dig deeper. Ask tough, direct questions about problem solving, past mistakes and how they take feedback. Look for ownership and hunger.
Face-to-face interview	This is make or break. The first twenty seconds tell you a lot, but the rest should confirm whether they: • Can handle pressure • Are aligned with your values • Bring energy to the room
Mini task or trial (if relevant)	Give them a task related to the role, something simple but real. It will reveal their work ethic and how they think.
Cultural fit test	Informally introduce them to other team members. Watch the dynamic. Do they mesh or feel out of place?

Give the process your time. It'll be worth it. You don't want to be in a situation of having a one-hour chat with the first person who applies, giving them a chance and then realising at the end of their first week that they are not right. It's a horrible feeling and a lot of hassle to undo. You will need to go through the rigorous process above with *at least* a dozen people, preferably many more. In fact, I wouldn't stop seeing people until exactly the right person is found.

You don't need to do all of this yourself. If you have a business partner on board, or a couple of trusted employees already in place, bring them into the process. I mentioned Poppy earlier, one of my business partners. Long before she took that role, she was one of my most trusted employees. When I was recruiting, I often asked her to carry out the telephone screening stage. She understood me, the company culture and what we were looking for. If Poppy was happy with the potential candidate and thought they might be a good fit, they'd be through to the next stage. We didn't do this for every role, but it helped to take the workload off me for some of them.

Next is the cultural fit test. I always try to get at least three or four of the team to meet promising candidates. This is a great way to see how they will all interact, how the applicant communicates and how they behave under pressure (there is a lot of pressure in a start-up).

You're not looking for someone who nods along and says 'yes' to everything. You are looking for a real person, with real opinions. Not that long ago, I was interviewing for a website developer and user experience designer. One candidate stood out, but he was also quite young, so I was keen to see how he'd interact with the rest of the team. He handled himself really well. He answered everyone's questions but, most importantly, he held his own. He didn't just agree with everyone. It was clear he'd be a good addition to the team and would bring a fresh perspective.

The interview process

The face-to-face interview is a key part of the process. To give yourself the best chance of landing the most suitable candidate, you need to make this stage less about ticking boxes and more about understanding the person behind the CV. The goal is to identify individuals who are not only qualified but who also resonate with your company's ethos and can contribute positively to the team dynamic. I prioritise authenticity and cultural fit over 'good' but rehearsed responses.

I always start by breaking the ice with a casual conversation. It doesn't have to be anything forced, just ask about their journey to the interview, or how their day has been so far. This approach helps candidates relax and can tell you a surprising amount about their natural demeanour.

Next, I start to delve into their background and aspirations, with questions like:

- 'Can you walk me through your previous roles and experiences?'

- 'What attracted you to this position and our company?'
- 'Where do you see yourself fitting into our team?'

These questions help to assess their relevant experience, their understanding of the company culture and their potential alignment with it. If they haven't even bothered to look at our website, it will be immediately obvious and a clear red flag that they are just keen on a job. Any job.

To gauge their true character and potential beyond the CV, I throw in some behavioural and situational questions designed to uncover their problem-solving skills, adaptability and interpersonal abilities:

- 'Can you describe a time when you faced a significant challenge at work? How did you handle it?'
- 'Tell me about a situation where you had to work closely with someone whose personality was very different from yours.'

Bear in mind that, while you want them to be articulate and thoughtful in their responses, it is not always about what they say, it's *how* they say it. Someone who's just after any job at all tends to give generic answers, show low energy and treat the interview like a box to tick. If someone wants *this* job, you'll feel it. They're engaged. They've done their homework. They ask smart questions. There's intent behind what they say. As we're talking, I'm constantly watching their body language and facial expressions. I'm not trying to convince anyone to join me. I'm looking for a spark. Does their face light up when they are talking about the business? Do they lean in? Do they start asking questions or throwing out ideas? Are they maintaining eye contact? That's how I know they're with me. You can tell when someone's excited, they can't help but show it. On the flip side, it's obvious when they're just nodding along, but not really feeling it.

One of the most telling moments for me is when the interview is over and the candidate leaves the room. The people who really want it, tend to leave a mark. They shake your hand properly, thank you with meaning and walk out like they're already part of the team. The ones who are just shopping around usually say little, leave fast and disappear without making a connection.

Qualities to prioritise

While their qualifications and experience are of course important, I'm always listening hard to what candidates say in the interview, looking for indicators of a few key qualities.

Belief

I need to know if they really *believe* in the mission, or if they're only interested in what they're going to get out of it personally. I understand that it's important to bring home a decent salary, but I don't want any passengers. In a start-up, belief is the most important thing. Your whole team needs to believe in you and your vision and trust that you'll get them there, and that the long hours and sacrifices are leading somewhere. If someone doesn't see what you're building as something bigger than just a job, they won't put in the effort when things get tough. You also don't want to be in the position of having to constantly convince someone of how brilliant your idea is. It's exhausting, and it never works.

Willingness

Closely related to belief is willingness. It sounds simple, but it's everything. I used to be blinded by experience, ticking boxes based on someone's CV. Now, I look deeper. Someone who's willing beats someone who's already done it, because in a start-up, what you've done before matters far less than what you're willing to do next. You need to see that they are going to be willing to show up, get their hands dirty and muck in whenever and wherever needed. Willingness is gold dust in an environment where things move fast, roles blur and problems don't come with instructions. I've seen experienced hires crumble under pressure because they weren't open to change. I've also seen someone with half the experience fly because they were hungry to learn and pushed themselves every day. You can tell if someone is willing by the questions they ask. If they are thoughtful and considered and show a lot of curiosity, that's a good sign.

Diversity

Remember, you are not looking to build a roomful of mini-mes. I talked about the importance of seeking complementary skills in a partnership, and the same goes for team members. Smart entrepreneurs create a team where everyone is a little different, with a good range of skillsets, approaches and viewpoints. Obviously, the various recruits need to be suitable for the job in hand. You don't want your finance person to be a free-wheeling ideas type; they've got to be into the fine detail with a laser focus. Nor do you want your salesperson to be an introverted, deep thinker. But you do want a mix of people who think differently. If you have a team who all have the same background and see things from the same angle, there'll be no fresh perspective, no challenge and no alternative solutions. This will slow you down.

On a similar note, think about the mix of the characters on the team. As you are listening to the candidate speak and watching their body language, think about how they'll fit in with the people already on the team in terms of their age, outlook on life and background. When I first started out, I always thought 'culture' was just some buzzword big corporations used. But the reality is, culture forms whether you try and put one in place or not. If you don't shape it, it'll shape itself – and in ways you might not like.

For example, in one of my early businesses I had a youngish team all from similar backgrounds. That made for a great, scrappy, start-up energy, but it also led to problems as lines got blurred between work and friendship. If everyone is too similar, accountability starts slipping and, before you know it, you're dealing with a business where no one knows who's actually in charge. A diverse mix of people makes for a much more stable, cohesive workplace.

Something else I look for is someone who will challenge my thinking and fill my gaps, not just agree with me all the time. I can, on occasion, get carried away with something that I think is a great idea but which, on closer examination, isn't quite so practical. I want someone to say, 'Hold on, I'm not sure about that' and then lay out their reservations. The reality is that no one is good at everything. You're not always going to have all the answers and if you try to do everything yourself while everyone nods in agreement, you'll limit your success. A strong team with diverse perspectives and experience will always outperform a solo entrepreneur.

When assessing at interview whether someone is likely to be an asset or a liability for my businesses, I look at the following.

Immediate indicators of a good fit

- **Authentic energy:** They walk in with a genuine enthusiasm, not over the top, but clearly indicating that they're excited about the opportunity.

- **Positive body language:** Open posture, consistent eye contact and a firm handshake suggest confidence and approachability.

- **Engaging communication:** They listen actively, respond thoughtfully and engage in the conversation without dominating it.

- **Cultural alignment:** Their demeanour and responses reflect your core values – grit, adaptability and a team-oriented mindset.

Red flags

- **Defensiveness:** If they react poorly to casual feedback or seem overly guarded, it may indicate difficulty with collaboration and growth.

- **Lack of enthusiasm:** A flat or disinterested demeanour can suggest they're not fully invested in the opportunity.

- **Incongruent communication:** If their words and body language don't align – for example, saying they're excited while appearing disengaged – it raises concerns about authenticity.

- **Overemphasis on personal gain:** Focusing too much on what they can get from the role, rather than what they can contribute, is a warning sign.

A two-way street

If you find someone who absolutely aces the interview and seems like the perfect fit, the chances are they will absolutely ace every interview with every company they meet with. Businesses will be falling over themselves to offer them a job. If you want the pick of the bunch, remember that interviewees are giving you the once-over too.

The knee-jerk reaction is to really sell the role. I don't do that. I focus on the mission. I talk about where the company is now, where we're heading and what the bigger picture looks like. I strip back the corporate fluff and give them the raw, unfiltered version of what we're building. I talk about the hustle, the challenges, the upside and what it'll take to get there. The idea is to make it compelling.

The right people don't just want a job; they want a mission they can believe in. By sharing my vision honestly and with energy, the people who are meant to be part of it will feel that. They'll buy in not because I sold it to them, but because what I said resonated with them. That, to me, is the real goal of hiring and building a brilliant team that will get things done. I want to find people who believe in what I'm building and who want to grow with me, not just professionally, but personally too. That kind of alignment is rare. When you find it, you hold on tight.

I also make sure to talk about the existing team and how much I value what they do. Good people are not just there for the money. Obviously, you need to pay them fairly, but what really keeps them around is knowing that they are valued. If you can't compete on salary, you must compete on something else. Maybe it's growth opportunities, or maybe it's ownership of a small stake in the business, but equally importantly, it's about them seeing that, if they join you, they will be heard and appreciated. Too many founders act like anyone who joins their team should feel lucky to have a job. That's wrong. You should feel lucky to have them. If you don't, they're probably the wrong hire.

Employment contracts

Once you get the right people in, the job isn't done. Contracts are just as important in hiring as they are in partnerships. Everything might look perfect on day one – everyone's excited, motivated and promising the world – but life happens. People's circumstances change. Maybe they suddenly need more money, more time at home, or just lose interest. If you don't have clear agreements in place from the start, it'll come back to bite you. I learned this the painful way when I had to let people go who weren't working out. Without solid contracts, it became a nightmare. Now, I make sure everything is watertight upfront.

It's human nature to push the limits, however well people come across at interviews and keen they sound. If you don't set clear rules, timelines and expectations, you're basically giving permission for standards to slip and pretty soon it is chaos. One person leaves early, another shows up late, someone else starts doing the bare minimum and, suddenly, the culture becomes 'do what you want, when you want'. When that happens, even the good people will either lower their standards to match, or they'll leave.

Having rock-solid contracts and six-month probation periods in place across the board should be non-negotiable. It's not about being controlling; it's about protecting what you're building. The probation period gives you time to properly test for culture fit and performance, while contracts make it clear what's expected and what isn't. No grey areas. No misunderstandings.

It might be tempting, as a start-up founder, to cut corners and write up something basic using a template, or copying and pasting from online. A junior member of the team is not as significant an investment as a business partner, right? No. Contracts aren't just paperwork or going through the motions. They're protection. They define the boundaries of the relationship, the expectations and your rights as a business owner. A DIY approach is not good enough. You'd be surprised by how much can be overlooked if you're not legally trained. If you miss something important, you'll only find out when it's too late.

As with the partnership agreement, I always recommend getting a professional involved in drawing up your employment contracts. Someone who knows employment law inside out. Yes, it might seem like a cost you don't need early on, but it's one of those things that pays for itself in the long run. There are affordable services out there, especially for start-ups, so do your research, find someone solid for a fair price and get your staff contracts sorted properly from day one. Once you've got a template you're happy with, you can reuse it, so you won't be starting from scratch every time. You just update the name, salary, job title and personal details, and you're good to go. In business, repeatable systems and templates will save you so much time and money.

8
A 360-Degree Team

Hiring the right people is one thing. Managing them is another. If you want to build something big, you can't just throw a bunch of people together, cross your fingers and hope they all get along and do their bit to make your business what you believe it can be. You need more than just staff; you need a real team.

To build an effective team, you need to keep in mind that working for a start-up is fundamentally different from working for an established company. Everyone you recruit will be stepping into an environment defined by speed, uncertainty and constant change. Unlike traditional roles in older companies, where responsibilities are clearly outlined and there is a strict hierarchy, start-ups often require people to wear multiple hats and adapt on the fly. Someone who is hired as a marketing assistant might end up contributing to product development, customer support or operations. The lines between roles are blurred, and people's ability to thrive often depends on their resourcefulness, flexibility and willingness to learn quickly. In contrast, established companies typically offer more predictable routines, formal hierarchies and clear career pathways. Processes are already in place, and each role is clearly defined and often pretty narrow in its purview. While this can provide stability and focus, it can also mean slower decision making and limited exposure to the broader business.

As a start-up founder, you can use these differences to your advantage. Everyone who works for you will be much closer to the core of every idea, and every problem and every win (and loss) will be felt more directly. This makes the work more intense, but also more personal. People are doing more than just a job; they're helping build the company from the ground up. That's exciting. The trick is to make everyone feel a part of it and that they personally can make a big difference. My tried and tested approach is to build what I call a 360-degree team.

The 360-degree philosophy

A 360-degree team is a group of individuals who are empowered to operate with full ownership, flexibility and accountability across a wide range of tasks, not just those outlined in their job description. In an environment where resources are tight and roles evolve quickly, a 360-degree team means everyone is able and prepared to jump in wherever they're needed. Instead of sticking to one title or function, it's about adopting a mindset where solving problems, supporting teammates and pushing the business forward is everyone's job, regardless of hierarchy or role.

What sets a 360-degree team apart is the sense of shared mission and mutual trust. No one is boxed into a rigid job description. Team members don't wait to be told what to do; they anticipate needs, offer ideas and take the initiative. A 360-degree team turns a start-up into a powerhouse of momentum, creativity and resilience. This culture only works when leadership makes a point of empowering people, valuing their input and treating them like partners. When done right, it's like having multiple business partners instead of employees.

There are other advantages, too. Once you've built this brilliant team, you'll want to hang on to them for as long as you can. It's tough to recruit the right people and bring them together into a close-knit team, so aim to build an environment where everyone sticks around for the long haul. Using this approach has meant a lot of the people who work for me have been with me for years and we've worked on multiple businesses together. I had the vision for each one, but my team made it a reality.

More than money

Believe it or not, in 360-degree teams there is a lot less focus on money and, let's face it, as a start-up you won't have much to offer either in salaries or perks. But for a 360-degree team member, money isn't everything. Money provides freedom, yes, but a sense of autonomy can't be bought with money alone. In my experience, this is the most powerful reason people stay with any of my companies: they value the freedom, culture and connection they feel every day at work.

Don't get me wrong, most of my team are on good salaries, but I genuinely believe that even if another company came along and offered them £5k or £10k more, they wouldn't jump ship. Why? Because, in my businesses, they have something that's harder to find than money: trust, autonomy and a sense of genuine belonging. They can get on with their jobs, are treated like adults and don't have someone breathing down their necks. Plus, they're empowered to make decisions, be creative and grow in their own way. That freedom creates ownership, and that ownership creates loyalty.

If someone on my team does get another offer, I'm pretty certain they'll tell me. That's how open the culture is. It has happened before; I've had team members come to me and say, 'Look, I've had another offer. This is what they're offering, and this is what I'm thinking.' Rather than getting defensive, I open the door to a proper conversation. They know they can speak honestly. If they feel they are underpaid, we talk about why, what they're looking for and whether there's a gap we can close. Most of the time, we come to an agreement, and they stay – not because I begged them to, but because they know they're valued.

If you can give your team even a taste of that – through flexibility, respect, a great culture and room to grow – they'll stick around, because what they have with you is worth more than what someone else could offer on paper. The grass isn't always greener. You can leave for more money and end up in a corporate environment where you're micromanaged, boxed in and surrounded by people you don't vibe with. I've heard so many stories from people who have left start-ups for higher salaries, only to find themselves in places where they felt like numbers, not people, just clocking in and out, and being monitored constantly. Most of us are looking for a sense of purpose and the freedom to live life on our terms.

The final advantage to building a 360-degree team is one for you personally, as the company founder: it will help you scale faster and better. If you are obsessive about every detail in your start-up, that's not surprising – it's your big idea and you want to make it fly. Yet, it's easy to fall into the trap of having your hands in everything, just to make sure. You start off that way before you have a team because you have to. But if you keep operating like that as you scale, you'll become the bottleneck. Things will slow down, decisions will pile up and progress will stall. Worst of all, you'll be disempowering and demotivating your team without even realising it, as well as creating a lot of unnecessary stress for yourself. Building a 360-degree team is the way to stop yourself from becoming that bottleneck. Be crystal clear on everyone's responsibilities, what you're trying to do and where you're trying to get to, and then *get out of the way*. Stay close enough to offer support where needed – you still need to be visible and on hand to give guidance – but far enough away to let people own their work. Things will change a lot as you scale, but the key is to enable everyone to get on with their job and to foster a culture that makes people want to contribute, not because they're told to, but because they care.

How to build a 360-degree team

The secret to building and maintaining an effective 360-degree team is to create a family dynamic. By family, I don't mean some cringey, awkward, fake-feeling corporate setup where executives at big firms call their staff 'family' while at the same time treating them like they're disposable. Nor am I suggesting everyone sits around holding hands. I'm talking about the way a real, well-functioning family works.

A 360-degree team is one that has each other's backs, moves as one and genuinely wants to see the business succeed, because they feel like an important part of it – which they are. There's a real sense of belonging and of showing up, not just because it's a job, but because everyone believes in what they're doing and who they're doing it with.

Early in my entrepreneurial journey, I made the mistake of viewing staff as easily replaceable. If someone didn't work out, I'd quickly hire someone else, assuming another person could simply fill the gap. But over time, I realised how flawed this mindset was and that I needed to invest time into creating the right culture.

Building my current team taught me the immense value of mutual respect and trust – between me and them, and between the individual team members. My team and I genuinely rely on each other: they depend on me for stability, income and opportunities, and I rely on their loyalty, dedication and productivity. I respect their contributions, consider their ideas and make them feel part of something meaningful. By shifting my approach from viewing employees merely as numbers or roles, to treating them as essential, valued individuals, I've created a team that consistently goes above and beyond.

Environment and culture

You need to create an environment where everyone feels good about one another because of a shared bond, rather like in a traditional family. This is the secret sauce that adds real energy to the team. You're aiming for a culture of openness and honesty, where people can speak frankly without others wondering if there is some coded subtext, or if they're just trying to get one over on them, which often happens in a cut-throat corporate environment.

I don't know about you, but when one of my close relatives promises to do something and then doesn't, someone else in the family will usually call them out – in a friendly way. It's the same in a 360-degree team. People hold each other accountable, not because they have to, or to backstab anyone, but because they want to protect what they're all building. Likewise, when someone is clearly buckling under the pressure trying to get a task done, their colleagues will immediately jump in to help. Everyone knows how hard everyone else is working and if they're not matching that energy, they'll feel it. That internal pressure and comradery, more than any formal job description, is what keeps standards high.

All culture is built from the top–down. As the founder of the company, you must model the behaviour you want to see and create an environment where the team feel invested in the business, rather than like hired hands. To achieve this, I include team members in everything. We talk openly, brainstorm together, I ask for their opinions, listen to their ideas and treat them like they actually matter because, guess what, they do. When you use a flat structure where input is welcome from any and every level, people feel included in the company ethos.

I am also careful not to pretend I know everything. Most of my team are younger than me, and that's a good thing. They think differently than I do. They see certain trends before I do, too. They also understand many platforms and technologies better than me. It makes sense, then, that I give them the freedom to speak up, challenge my thinking and run with their own ideas. If I were arrogant enough to think I had all the answers, I'd have missed out on some of the best things that have happened in my businesses.

> **Hustle mindset tips for building and maintaining a 360-degree team**
>
> - **Value and respect your team:** Employees aren't just numbers. Genuine respect and appreciation foster loyalty, productivity and commitment.
> - **Encourage open communication:** Create an environment where team members feel safe sharing ideas. Innovative solutions can come from within the team, not just leadership.
> - **Consistency builds loyalty:** Frequent staff turnover negatively impacts productivity, morale and your bottom line. Building long-term relationships creates stability and efficiency.
> - **Listen and adapt:** Recognise your limitations as a leader. Being open to your team's insights and willing to adapt demonstrates true leadership strength and significantly enhances team performance.

Creating a family dynamic will require a mindset shift. While you are understandably keen to get on with the task of scaling up, you need to remember it can't all be work, work, work. Like all families, you will need some time to relax and unwind together and enjoy each other's company. This should happen outside of the workplace, or there will be a temptation for people to sneak back to their desks.

It doesn't have to be anything formal. 'We'll be having a pub night next Tuesday at The Feathers from 8pm,' is more the vibe. Team building shouldn't be forced. It's much better when it happens naturally. For example, a lot of my team go to events together, like weekend barbeques, or have impromptu trips to the pub on quieter days. This is the way to build real friendships, not just work relationships. I honestly think some of the people on my team would be gutted not to see each other every day. That kind of bond only forms when the culture is genuine and people feel safe being themselves.

Let me give you a small, but powerful, example of how this kind of culture builds exceptional relationships. We've got a team member called Alex. Every single morning, without being asked, she goes to the shop and buys fresh fruit for the team. This is off her own back, with her own money. It's not about the fruit. It's about the thought. She quietly sets the tone for the day by doing something generous and community minded. That's what a family-style culture looks like in practice – people going above and beyond for each other without expecting anything in return.

In start-ups, the work is hard and the hours can be long. Yet, when your team feels like a unit, like a real support system, people tend to stick around. That's when they go the extra mile, not because they're told to, but because they want to.

Disruptors

Let's face it, we don't live in a perfect world. Things do change, and sometimes for the worse. Maybe someone you bring in after a thorough interview process doesn't work out as you'd hoped and starts to chip away at the close bonds your team have built. Someone who was previously a model worker may just lose interest or become distracted due to external circumstances, for example a sick relative at home, or issues with childcare. They might not flag it immediately, but simply start slipping away earlier and earlier each day. I had an example of this with an executive assistant who kept leaving before 5pm, while the rest of the team stayed long afterwards. That kind of behaviour didn't just break a rule, it broke the culture. Sure, some days we let the whole team leave early, but that's done openly, through the managers, as a collective decision. The moment someone starts living by their own rules, it disrupts the group energy. Everyone will notice, and it will start to erode trust, morale and accountability. Over time, this can create resentment and dysfunction.

In my current business, we've built a culture where hard work, ownership and pride in the mission are the norm; if anyone is not pulling their weight it sticks out. If someone's coasting while everyone else is grafting, it becomes obvious quickly. When we had the issue with the executive assistant, it wasn't me who raised it; it was the other team members, not management, who pulled me aside and said, 'so-and-so's not really putting in the effort'. That wasn't snitching; it was respect for the business. That's a team that cared about the standard we'd all set together.

Ultimately, though, it is up to leadership to flag and curb any poor behaviour or drop in performance. Which brings me to one of the inherent dangers of a family dynamic: being too close to your team. It is possible for founders to lose objectivity. When strong personal relationships override professional boundaries, it becomes harder to make tough calls, give honest feedback or deal with conflict.

If you are leading a 360-degree team, maintaining discipline can feel like a delicate task. After all, you've exerted all that energy creating a family atmosphere and spending time with everyone. It's important that a leader leads with empathy, but not emotion. Yes, you can and should care deeply about the team, but you must always put the business and its standards first.

Leading a 360-degree team comes down to striking a balance between approachability and authority. A strong leader sets the tone, expectations and culture, but also knows when to step back and let the team take ownership and when to draw a line and call out bad behaviour. It is absolutely possible to be open, empathetic and involved in the day-to-day without blurring the lines. The way to do this is to have real conversations, listen actively and give credit where it's due, while also letting it be known that you will be holding people accountable, making hard decisions and calling out underperformance when needed. Respect isn't built by being liked; it's built by being consistent, fair and clear about the standards the whole team lives by.

You don't need to lose your head or make a scene. You just need to take aside the person who isn't pulling their weight and have a direct conversation. Say something like: 'Look, this isn't on. It's not fair to the rest of the team and it's not how we do things here.' Usually, that's enough. If it isn't, you'll need to have some tougher conversations – there may even need to be some changes to the team.

That's why leadership matters. *You* set the tone. If you let things slide, allow excuses and don't make hard decisions, the team will mirror that. I had to learn to be ruthless, not in a cut-throat way, but in setting standards. You have to reward the people who put in the effort and cut ties with those who don't. It's tough, but keeping the wrong people around drags down the ones who actually care. It can also create a bad atmosphere. Accountability isn't about being strict; it's about keeping the playing field level. Fairness keeps trust intact.

Trust, celebration and shared wins

Having talked about the stick, let's end on the carrot. You rise as a team, or not at all. While you should absolutely crack down when someone is taking the proverbial, you need to be just as quick to celebrate the wins. This only works if you give credit where it's due. Too many business owners take all the praise when something goes well and are quick to shift the blame when it doesn't. That's a quick way to lose your best people. When we succeed, it's because of *us*, not just me. I make sure that everyone on my team knows that. It's another way to build trust, and trust is everything when you're working at the kind of speed we do.

Never lose sight of the fact that loyalty and dedication in your team is something you need to nurture. Make sure they feel valued and secure and they will pay this loyalty back in kind. This is particularly noticeable during the challenging periods that inevitably arrive for any ambitious start-up. There were times when my team faced uncertainty about whether the business would be able to make the payroll, yet their loyalty never wavered. This is something I've made sure to recognise. As well as making sure I communicated our situation openly whenever things looked bad, I also acknowledged their contribution when we came out the other side. I rewarded their loyalty by involving them more closely in the business's success, granting each team member a small stake in key ventures. As I mentioned, money isn't everything, but this created alignment between their success and the business's overall performance. It also had an energising impact, making subsequent decisions stronger, more innovative and better tailored to the marketplace.

Loyalty comes from showing trust, openness and care, especially during uncertain times. Giving team members ownership in the form of bonuses, profit shares and equity builds long-term commitment. When the good times roll around – which they will, thanks to your brilliant team – be sure to give credit and reward where it is due.

9
The Quiet Power Of Solid Systems And Processes

Every business, without exception, has its problems. Even the 'most successful' ones. From the outside, you might see the big wins, the polished success stories and the headlines about record-breaking revenues and billion-pound valuations. What you don't see is the chaos behind the scenes: the supply chain issues, the late payments, the contracts gone wrong, the unexpected tax bills and the founder's 2am panic attacks when something major goes sideways. Every business, no matter how good it looks from the outside, is dealing with its own pile of shit. The trick isn't finding a way to avoid it. You can't. You need to learn how to manage it, so it doesn't drag you under. The best way to do that? Systems and processes.

I see so many start-ups getting this wrong. They're busy hustling, signing up clients and bringing in sales, but there's no structure. For example, they don't have a proper invoicing system, they're not tracking payments and don't have a contract process. It's just a free-for-all of deals made over WhatsApp and through verbal agreements that come back to bite them later. They're running at full speed but leaving a trail of mess behind them and, sooner or later, that mess needs cleaning up.

Get your house in order

Remember the figure I quoted earlier about half of new businesses failing within the first five years? For the majority of these, it's not because the founder had a rubbish idea; they fail because they don't have their house in order. You can have the best idea ever and be the best salesperson in the world, but if you're not tracking your jobs, chasing invoices and making sure your payment terms are solid, you're setting yourself up for disaster. If you're not systematic about the money coming in and processing it properly, you won't survive. It's that simple.

But it's not just about survival. Systems and processes are what makes your business valuable. Selling your company might feel like a distant dream right now, but whether you sell in five years or twenty, the things that make your business sellable are the same things that keep it running smoothly day to day. Investors and buyers don't just look at your revenue; they look at how organised the business is. They want to see clear processes, airtight contracts and reliable financial tracking. If they find a mess, they'll walk away, no matter how impressive your sales figures are. The same goes for a business where the founder does everything themselves and all the important stuff is in his or her head. Who wants to buy a business like that? All the value in that business is with the founder, who would be walking away with a big payout once they'd sold the business – so it would never happen.

If your end goal is to sell your business, whether that's to cash out, step back, or just move on to the next thing, then you've got to start building it like an asset. From day one, you want to be making decisions that increase the value of the company, not just short-term profits.

Zoom in

I think the reason most entrepreneurs overlook things like systems and processes is because of how we're wired. A lot of entrepreneurs, me included, are creative, high-energy, forward-thinking types. When we're locked in and focused on an idea, we go all in. We get into that flow state, chasing opportunities, solving problems and creating. That's the part we love. It's what we're here for. When you're starting out and deep into that flow, it's tempting to just wing it, keep everything in your head, chase payments manually and ad hoc and dig around for files when needed. But when you end up wearing every hat – product, sales, marketing, finance – and trying to spin all those plates, something will get neglected and catch up with you later. Usually, it's the boring-but-crucial stuff like chasing invoices or setting up proper payment structures. It just doesn't seem urgent until it's a problem.

Trust me, discipline early on saves stress later. In my early businesses, I was so focused on the big wins that I let the backend slip. I had clients, I had revenue, but I also had unpaid invoices piling up, missed follow-ups and a growing pile of headaches. I had to fix things, fast. Now, every business I build runs like a machine. Every contract is solid, every payment is tracked and every process is in place before we scale. It's not the exciting part of business, but it's the part that keeps you in business.

This might all feel a bit daunting, but it doesn't need to be. A few years ago, this sort of thing required a lot more time and effort. Today, AI and modern tech can take on so much of the burden. Yes, you'll have to put in a bit of effort to set it all up, but then it will be plain sailing. Once it's done, your business will be built on a firm foundation. I'm amazed that so many SMEs are still reliant on models that could have been built thirty, forty, even fifty years ago. Too many entrepreneurs cling to outdated systems, or worse, launch without any tech at all. Today, technology isn't just an add-on, it's the engine that drives your business. In our current era, businesses cannot afford to move slowly. We've left the industrial age behind. This is the digital revolution and those who move fast, adapt, and integrate technology will win.

Before you start making serious money, there are two core groups of systems and processes every new business should have in place from day one: one to look after the finances, and one to make sure everything else at the backend is running smoothly so that you can focus on getting and delivering for new customers. In other words, you need to manage your money and manage your clients. There are also a few miscellaneous bits of tech that just make your life a million times easier. It's not glamorous, but it's foundational.

Managing the money

Financial hygiene is a difficult thing to get right in any business, especially when you're in that early or scaling phase. You're constantly being pulled toward growth, juggling new clients, new opportunities, bigger deals and moving fast to scale up. That's the fun bit, where you feel like you're building something. At the same time, if you take your eye off cash flow and operations, you can 'grow' yourself straight into the ground. It's not just about making money; it's about keeping it, managing it and making sure your business can handle the weight of its own growth.

Again, I've been there. You land a few big deals and you're flying, already thinking about the next move. Behind the scenes, though, if the cash isn't flowing, or if your systems and team can't keep up, cracks will start to show. Sure, you might be growing on paper, but inside the business, things will be chaotic. Invoices will get sent out late, a few maybe even missed altogether, delivery dates will slip, service quality drops and, suddenly, that growth you were chasing will cost you more than it's worth. All of this is before you get to the point of forgetting to file or pay your Corporation Tax or VAT on the right date. No business wants to get on the radar of HMRC.

Even if you're only dealing with a handful of clients, the way you manage your money and operations reflects how serious you are about the business. For me, it's about layering in discipline as you go. You can – and should – still be aggressive with your growth ambitions, but you must stay grounded. That means:

- Watching cash flow like a hawk. Not only revenue, but also what's actually coming in and going out each week.

- Having proper payment terms and systems in place to chase any late payments of invoices, so you're not always playing catch-up.

- Making sure your team, tools and processes can scale with you, rather than being liable to break under pressure.

You don't need to overcomplicate it, but you do need to be disciplined.

What, then, are the tools you should be using? The first thing you need is an invoice and accounting system. This is software that helps you stay on top of cash flow, track expenses, manage invoices and avoid the mess that comes from mixing up your money. It doesn't matter if you're only making a few hundred pounds a month, build good habits from the start ready for when you are earning tens of thousands. If you don't know your numbers, you don't know your business. We use Xero, but there are plenty of other products on the market, some of which might suit you better. The table below lists some that are worth checking out, along with a summary of their key features.

For accounting software, pricing tends to be dependent upon the service level plan you choose and the number of users. They all offer low-cost starter plans, and some even have free trials or discounts for start-ups. Once you sign up, all these products are easy to set up yourself, even if you have no bookkeeping or accounts knowledge. You simply input your details and then off you go. It should go without saying, but you need to keep up with the admin – ie make sure you input payments and regularly reconcile your bank feeds to record income and outgoings.

Once set up, the tech makes the day-to-day accounting easy. You can, for example, automate recurring invoices, or set up monthly retainers. You can also enable automatic payment reminders for overdue invoices, or make use of integrated payment links like Stripe or PayPal, to ensure funds hit your account more quickly. The mobile apps that come with these systems can also be handy. You can use your phone to capture receipts and instantly upload them to add to expenses, or send an invoice on the go.

Accounting tools

Tool	Type of business suited for	Best features	Integrations
Xero	Growing SMEs, start-ups, limited companies	• Highly customisable, with features such as multicurrency, inventory and project tracking • Great for start-ups seeking investment, with strong audit trail and reporting	PayPal, Stripe, Spotify, HubSpot
QuickBooks	Retailers, sole traders and service-based businesses	• Clean user experience, good for those with no bookkeeping experience • Best for managing day-to-day sales, expenses, mileage and basic payroll	Amazon, eBay, PayPal, Revolut
FreeAgent	Freelancers, contractors and micro-businesses	• Clear tax dashboard and timeline • Automatically calculates income tax, VAT and dividend payouts (for limited companies)	HMRC, NatWest, Starling, PayPal

Sage Accounting	Traditional businesses, professional services firms and established SMEs	• Strong financial reports, accrual vs cash accounting support • Good for businesses with an in-house finance admin, or which require external accountant involvement	Microsoft 365, PayPal, Stripe
Zoho Books	Tech-savvy start-ups, digital agencies or SaaS companies	• Seamless integration with Zoho suite of products (CRM, Projects, Desk and custom automation) • Good value for small teams with time tracking and workflow features	Zoho CRM, G Suite, PayPal, Stripe
Crunch	Freelancers, contractors and micro-businesses	• Dedicated accountant through app • Integrated invoicing, expense tracking and bank feeds • Built in VAT submissions and dividend planning tools	HMRC integration and bank feeds

Finally, and this is important, if everything is kept up to date, you've got a ready-made dashboard full of data to keep tabs on key metrics like unpaid invoices and cashflow trends, and upcoming tax deadlines.

Managing the backend

Chaos kills a business. While founders thrive on energy, speed and vision, without structure, all that potential quickly gets overwhelming. As I've found to my cost, it is easy to overlook small, but essential details (like cyber security – more on that shortly), but there are other elements in the less dramatic backend of a business that you need to attend to. Just as a brilliant idea can easily collapse under the weight of disorganisation, a growing customer base can also become a liability when follow-ups are neglected, emails go unanswered and delivery timelines are missed.

Early signs that your backend is in chaos and you're potentially losing hard-earned business are:

- A spreadsheet full of half-finished leads
- A to-do list scattered across five different apps
- A team unclear on who's doing what, or when it's due
- A customer frustrated because they have to explain their problem again

In the short term, it's survivable. The very short term. Quickly, this sloppiness at the backend can cost you everything and bring down the business. Momentum keeps your business moving forward, but chaos interrupts that flow. It will force you into being constantly reactive, pulling focus away from strategy and growth. Without systems to keep everything running smoothly at the backend, every win demands more energy, more oversight and more time – all the stuff you've been using up trying to grow the business. If your business depends entirely on you remembering, doing and fixing, everything, it's not a business, it's a bottleneck. Well, to be more accurate, you've become the bottleneck.

Backend systems and processes will save you. Using the right tools and apps will protect your momentum by ensuring consistency, clarity and control. At the very least, I would adopt systems for client relationship management (CRM), project management and internal comms. I would also make use of some of the brilliant AI tools out there, as they just make everything a lot easier. I've put them in a 'misc' section because they cover so many bases. Let's take each in turn.

Client relationship management (CRM)

A CRM system is your command centre for managing contacts, leads, client interactions and follow-ups. You can store notes, set reminders and track conversations, all in one place. This is important when trying to build strong relationships with customers, because you can see at a glance what they've bought, what they've asked about and what they might need in the future. You can use all this information to track sales pipelines, set reminders and automate follow-ups, so deals can be closed with a lot less effort. These systems are so cheap now. You can get solid, off-the-shelf CRMs for free, or at a very low cost per user. So there's no excuse; if you're not tracking conversations and follow-ups, you're leaving money on the table. A CRM system keeps everything organised, saving you a ton of time and ensuring no opportunities are missed.

CRM tools

Tool	Best suited for	Key features
HubSpot CRM	Start-ups and small businesses looking for a free, scalable tool	• User-friendly • Email tracking • Basic automation
Zoho CRM	Small to mid-sized businesses needing customisation	• Custom modules • Analytics • AI features
Pipedrive	Sales-focused teams wanting simplicity and speed	• Visual pipelines • Sales tracking • Automation
Salesforce Essentials	Growing businesses needing robust features and scalability	• Advanced reporting • Automation • Lead scoring
Capsule CRM	Freelancers and small teams needing simple integrations	• Simple UI • Contact management • Task tracking

It'll take a little time to get your head around whichever of these tools you go for, but it will be time well spent. The thing to remember is that a CRM system isn't just a fancy contacts list. If you use it properly, it can become the heartbeat of your business.

To give you a simple example of how CRM works, let's say a prospect fills out an enquiry form on your website. In many businesses, that just pings in as an email, which can easily be lost in an overflowing inbox. When you've got a CRM tool connected, that enquiry automatically creates a new lead in the system, along with the person's name, contact details, company and anything else you've asked for. This means you don't have to fiddle around creating a new prospect to record manually, or risk forgetting altogether. You can also set it up so that a new lead is instantly assigned to a team member, making them accountable for it. After that, every interaction is stored under that client's profile: notes, call logs, documents, contracts and even KYC (Know Your Customer) checks. If someone on your team spoke to the client last week, you'll be able to see exactly what was discussed. Some CRMs even go further. For instance, HubSpot can record phone calls, transcribe them automatically and save the transcript to the client file. If there's ever a 'he said, she said' dispute, you've then got the proof in writing.

Project management and internal comms

If you're juggling lots of different tasks or working with a team, you need tools that help you to stay on top of what's going on. Resolving to just email each other with important requests is not sustainable and things will get missed. Don't ever put yourself in a position of relying on messy group chats or disjointed email threads. Clear comms means less confusion.

Project management tools

Tool	Best suited for	Best features
Trello	Simple task tracking for individuals and small teams	• Visual Kanban boards • Task checklists • Due dates
ClickUp	Start-ups and growing teams needing flexible workflows	• Highly customisable tasks • Time tracking • Detailed lists and docs
Google Workspace	Businesses wanting a full suite of productivity tools	• Docs • Sheets • Slides • Gmail • Meet integration
Slack	Real-time team communication and file sharing	• Channels • Threads • Integrations • Real-time chat
Asana	Teams managing projects with timelines and dependencies	• Timeline view • Automation • Task dependencies
Notion	Creative teams needing docs and databases	• All-in-one workspace • Templates • Rich content blocks

Tool	Best suited for	Best features
Microsoft Teams	Organisations needing deep Microsoft integration	• Video calls • Chat • Calendar integration • File sharing

Misc

As I am sure you have realised by now, time and focus are among the most precious resources any founder has. We'll come back to that in more detail in the next chapter. In the meantime, let's look at the tech that can keep you on track. Anything you can get your hands on that will save you time is worth its weight in gold and, thanks to AI, there are loads of tools that can do just that. Ignore them at your cost. Below are a bunch of great tools that will help eliminate busywork, automate repetitive tasks and enhance creativity or communication, helping you to do more with less. These tools are invaluable to entrepreneurs today, who are often wearing multiple hats – marketer, designer, strategist, customer service rep – all at once, while trying to compete with the big players. These tools level the playing field by giving small businesses access to capabilities once reserved for large teams in established enterprises. For any entrepreneur looking to scale with limited resources, this is what you need for survival and success.

Miscellaneous tech tools for business

Tools	Best suited for	Best features
ChatGPT	Content creation, idea generation, research and problem solving	• Conversational AI • Content drafting • Brainstorming • Coding help • Summarising documents
Canva	Designing brand assets, pitch decks and social content	• Templates • Drag and drop editor, looks professional with minimal effort • Brand kits • Collaboration
Grammarly	Writing support, grammar improvement, tone suggestions	• Grammar checking • Real-time editing
Loom	Screen recording for tutorials, pitches or updates	• Instant video sharing • Webcam and screen recording • Analytics
Otter.ai	Transcribing meetings, interviews and audio notes	• Live transcription • Speaker ID • Searchable transcripts
Notion AI	AI-powered document writing, planning and summarising	• AI-assisted writing task summaries • Action item generation
Copy.ai	Creating marketing copy and product descriptions quickly	• Marketing-focused templates • Blog ideas • Email campaigns

When you're bootstrapping, the biggest mistake you can make is to leave sorting all the backend stuff out for later. Unfortunately, 'later' usually means after you've lost clients or let money slip through the cracks. All the tools in this section and the previous ones are dirt cheap compared to the cost of disorganisation. You could easily run your early-stage business for less than you probably spend on your personal phone bill, plus dip in and out of all the misc tools when needed. That's less than what many people spend on takeaways. It sets the tone: that your business is legit, trackable and professional, even if it's currently just you in your bedroom making it happen.

The lists I've shared here are all the platforms I'd recommend, either because we've used them ourselves, or they're just solid, no-nonsense tools that give you the most bang for your buck. Give them a try and get set up now, while your business is in its early stages. Start lean, stay organised and let these tools support your hustle.

Cyber security

After running through all the great tech tools and platforms out there that can support you on your business journey, I'd like to close this chapter with a word on cyber security.

Cyber security is not just a nice to have – it is essential for most business. I have a story – well, more of a cautionary tale – that should drive this point home. It's about a business based on an idea that was genuinely clever. It was one of those rare, clean solutions to a problem that people had just been quietly putting up with for years. It all started with a simple observation: the training industry was broken.

You'll remember me talking about Trusted Training 4U, the training business I founded, which delivered training either face-to-face, sending instructors out to client sites, or online through a third-party platform. Once up and running, we found a real issue with freelance instructors. I'd send them out on a job and there was about a 30% chance that, after a few sessions, the client would quietly cut us out. They'd start booking the trainer directly for follow-up training sessions. There was leak in the business model. Everyone wants to save a bit of money and freelance trainers were happy to pocket more by cutting out the middleman – us. I've seen it happen in other industries too. Walk into any gym and you'll hear the same story. The gym's trainers will quietly offer sessions 'off the books' for half the price if you pay them directly, bypassing the gym altogether. And it's not worth the gym pursuing it – it would cost more in legal fees than they'd ever get back. The same was true at Trusted Training 4U. It just wasn't worth the time trying to get the freelancers to stop it.

Then, one day, the idea hit me. What if there was a Checkatrade for trainers? I was thinking of a proper platform where freelance trainers could list their services for food safety training, first aid, care certificates – everything. Clients could log on, browse qualified trainers near them, check reviews and hire them directly. The freelance trainers would pay a monthly subscription to be listed, set their own rates and handle their own bookings.

It was a win–win. Clients would save money because they weren't paying middleman fees, meanwhile, trainers would make more because they were cutting out the agency markup. Most importantly for me, we, as the platform owners, would make money from the subscriptions. We didn't need to stop at listings, either. The platform could handle invoicing, payment processing and admin. Trainers could generate invoices directly through the site and we'd take a 10% commission on each job, in addition to the subscription fees. It was simple, scalable and I already had a database of 1,400 trainers from Trusted Training 4U ready to go.

I partnered with Chris, a tech guy I'd worked with for years who already ran an online training company. He knew the digital side and I knew the training industry inside out. Between us, it was the perfect setup. The build took about a year, but by the end of that time we'd created a proper, scalable product that could disrupt the training industry.

What I didn't know then was that we had a massive blind spot. Neither of us were thinking about cybersecurity. Like so many entrepreneurs, we were completely focused on the front end, thinking about the product, marketing and user experience. Meanwhile, the entire platform – every bit of code, every user record, every feature – was being built live on Chris's servers. There were no backups. No redundant servers. No off-site copies. We wrongly assumed the backend would take care of itself.

One day, out of nowhere, Chris's entire server infrastructure got hacked. Everything we'd built vanished. At the time, Chris had been having problems with other training companies and was convinced that the cyber-attack wasn't random. Whether or not that was true didn't make any difference because, just like that, a whole year's worth of work and thousands of lines of code were gone.

Obviously, we were gutted, but I learned a valuable lesson too: you can build the best product in the world, but if you don't protect it, that doesn't matter. We entrepreneurs love focusing on the exciting stuff – the branding, marketing, product features and the launch. But the unsexy stuff? Server security, backups, firewalls and threat monitoring? We often leave that until later. Or in our case, until it was too late.

If your business involves holding people's data, or handles any sort of financial transaction online, you need to invest in cyber security. Not only could you lose everything following a cyber-attack, like I did, but you'll also be vulnerable to getting sued if there is a data leak.

Don't assume that you'll most likely be OK. It's happening more and more. More than a quarter of UK businesses (27%) have reported experiencing cyber-attacks and those numbers are rising every year.[5]

---

5   J Kollewe, 'More than 25% of UK businesses hit by cyber-attack in last year, report finds', *The Guardian* (30 June 2025), www.theguardian.com/business/2025/jun/30/uk-businesses-hit-by-cyber-attack-last-year-report, accessed December 2025

THE QUIET POWER OF SOLID SYSTEMS AND PROCESSES

As well as regular backups, you need to ensure data is stored securely and install malware protection. Making sure you are properly protected is not something you can handle yourself. It is a wise investment to bring in a professional to advise on and manage your cyber security and regularly conduct cyber risk assessments to check for vulnerabilities. You don't need to spend a fortune. Take a view based on what your business does and then see what the experts say.

10
Time Waits For No One

Imagine your first business is flying. Money is coming in, your team is growing and you start thinking, *I've got this*. So you do what any ambitious entrepreneur would do, you start another business. Maybe even another. This is where I have to throw in a 'health and sanity warning': spreading yourself too thin can be a killer. And, yes, once again, I learned this the hard way.

Do you remember Jane and the findom business I talked about in Chapter 5? Well, that didn't work out as I hoped and became a huge drain on my time – just when I needed to be on top of my game.

What went wrong? From the beginning, Jane made a lot of bold claims about what she could bring to the table: her network, her experience in the adult industry and how she'd be pushing the platform twenty-four-seven once it was live. On paper, it sounded like a great partnership and a solid plan, which is why I decided to move forward and started investing (a lot of) time and money into building the platform.

As things moved forward, it became clear that Jane wasn't going to deliver. To begin with, there were a few red flags, but they quickly piled up. She started making excuses for not delivering things I'd asked for, was defensive whenever I chased them up and then would tell obvious lies about what she was doing (or not doing, to be more accurate). It got to a point where I had to call her out and hold her to what she'd said she was going to do.

But instead of stepping up or even having an honest conversation about what was going on, she completely shut down. She walked away from the project and blocked me on WhatsApp. She left me holding everything – the platform, the company and the pressure – with no one to drive it forward. Bear in mind, I had already invested a decent amount of money and nearly two years of my time into the build. To make things worse, I had payment processors chasing for updates and all I could do was relay what Jane had told me, but because her information was unreliable and, as it turned out, incorrect, it made me look dishonest. This sort of thing can seriously damage your credibility, especially in high-risk industries where trust with processors is everything.

There I was, with a live platform but no one to front it, damaged trust behind the scenes and a project that was about to fall apart right before launch. It is impossible to quantify how much time I spent trying to unravel it all – to the detriment of my other businesses. I was lucky that I had an amazing team behind me who kept everything else on track.

Before I go into the detail of time management, let me just share that this story did have a happy ending. When it all looked close to collapse, I reached out to a few contacts. I didn't want to bring in just anyone to fill the gap. I needed someone I trusted both personally and professionally, who could take this seriously and deliver. I spoke to Olivia, a friend of mine who runs a successful jewellery business `and someone who I've always respected for being hardworking and reliable. During our conversation, I explained what had happened with Jane and how the project had stalled. By complete chance, Olivia mentioned Megan, someone she knew who was already thinking about building a platform to empower creators. Megan, being a creator herself, understood exactly what this industry needed: a safe, supportive community, built by creators, for creators. The timing couldn't have been better. I already had the foundation, technical build and infrastructure, but I was missing an authentic voice and vision from within the creator community. Olivia introduced us and everything immediately clicked.

Megan and I were completely aligned from the start. She had the insight and experience from a creator's perspective, and I had the technical and business know-how needed to scale the platform. Together, we were able to turn what had been a stressful, draining experience into a genuine opportunity. The platform found its purpose again and, this time, it was built on mutual trust, shared values and a genuine understanding of the people it was designed for.

What started off as a nightmare with broken promises, wasted time and a bad partnership that nearly derailed the entire setup, ended up becoming one of the best things that could have happened. I've now got a stronger setup, better connections and a much clearer route forward.

This story ended better than I could have hoped, but it could easily have been a disaster. Looking back, I know exactly where I went wrong. Diversification is great, but it is time-consuming and must be done carefully. If one business starts draining the life out of another – or worse, draining you – then it's not growth, it's a distraction and not an efficient use of your time.

The biggest mistake entrepreneurs make is thinking they can handle everything and that their time is limitless. In reality, your time is finite. It's your most valuable asset and, if you don't protect it, you'll lose control. Through the experience described above, and others, I've had to learn to watch my time like a hawk, to stay focused and organised and to listen when my team tell me something isn't working or isn't worth it. If you're too busy to act quickly when there are warning signs, you risk missing them completely. I had a lucky break with Olivia and Megan, but I had lost control over my own time and it could have been game over.

'Busy' doesn't mean 'successful'

Time management is one of those things that everyone wants to master, but few manage. It is especially important when you're first starting out in business because you don't always have the luxury of perfect schedules and neatly organised days. In the early stages of any business, you'll be spinning a lot of plates, wearing different hats and dealing with a hundred things at once. You'll be handling sales, marketing, customer service and admin. It will all be on you. You'll try to manage your time efficiently, but the truth is, it's not always that easy. But being busy and being productive are two completely different things.

Anyone can be busy. You can wake up every day and be flat-out, jumping from one task to the next, replying to messages, putting out fires, ticking off to-do lists – but that doesn't mean you're achieving anything meaningful. Good time management comes down to having clear direction: knowing exactly where you're going, what you're doing and why you're doing it. When you don't have a vision, or a strong 'why', it's easy to mistake being busy for making progress. If you don't have a properly articulated plan or end goal, you end up chasing noise instead of results. You might feel like you're working hard, but hard work in the wrong direction is wasted effort.

Aside from lack of a clear direction, the other reason some founders get distracted is ego. They love the idea of being an entrepreneur and may show off a little, playing to the crowd: 'Yeah, I have a start-up and am talking to investors about a £1 million valuation...' I've seen a lot of people in the business world make decisions about how to spend their time purely based on ego, and it never ends well. They want to be right, to be seen and to get the 'win', even if it's not the right move for the business. That's not leadership. That's short-sighted, and a waste of their time.

On the flip side to unproductive 'busy-ness', running out of steam, or getting complacent, is another way you can waste time.

Don't let yourself drift

All being well, after a good amount of grafting and with a bit of luck, your business will start to fly. You'll get to the point where you're not constantly stressed about whether the bills can be paid. You'll even be able to take some proper cash out of the business. This can be a moment of danger. When you have a bit more of it, if you're not laser focused on how you use your time, a terrible thing will happen: you'll start coasting.

I did this myself, not long after the COVID pandemic. I'd picked myself up from all the disruption and, even though it hadn't been easy, got all my businesses back on track. Then, without really noticing, I took my foot off the gas and started plodding along. The office seemed to be running itself well enough, so I wasn't as hands-on as I usually like to be. I wasn't pushing growth or constantly looking for the next opportunity. While everything looked fine on the surface, it wasn't. I was not using my time well and things began to stagnate.

I wasted two years in that comfortable rut. Two years when I could have been growing my businesses. The crazy thing is, I didn't even fully realise it until one day it just hit me: I was a bit bored. Actually, I was *really* bored.

I sat there and thought: *What the f**k am I doing?*

I was tired, out of shape and I wasn't in the office enough. My team, to their credit, had kept things moving, even though they were a bit mystified at the lack of direction. But things had started to noticeably drift, because the energy was gone. I'd built this life for freedom, not to indulge in laziness, mediocrity or wasting my days, yet I was allowing everything to slowly crumble and letting everybody down.

This realisation was the rocket I needed. I snapped out of it and was able to bring everything back to where it should be and, business-wise, it was a transformational moment. The key to putting everything right was watching and managing my time like a hawk.

I'm conscious that managing your time is a lot easier said than done. I am 100% focused on my businesses and have been around the block a few times, but I still make mistakes with my time, as the findom example at the start of this chapter shows. It is easy to get distracted.

If you feel that you might not be using your time to best effect, do this simple test. Stop and ask yourself:

- What have I moved forward in the last month?
- Is my business bringing in revenue?
- Am I building anything that's growing or improving?
- What have I been doing that hasn't made any difference?

If your answers reveal that you're not maximising your time and energy – don't worry. In the next section, I'll share with you the tips and tricks I use to stay on track with my time. These are simple things that you can easily make a part of your routine.

How to best use your time and resources

When you're starting out, there's no escaping the fact that you will have to do a bit of everything. That's why it's even more important to prioritise managing your time wisely. If you don't, you'll spend your whole day being busy without getting anywhere.

Be strategic

Success comes from being intentional and focusing your time on the stuff that moves the needle, even if it's less exciting or doesn't give you that dopamine hit. Being smart and strategic with your time means having tunnel vision, always looking towards the bigger picture and focusing on quality over quantity. This means doing the things that lead to money on the board, deals closed, systems built and momentum gained, not surface-level activity. Even if you're making a loss, there should be cash coming in and measurable traction. If you're constantly busy but nothing's shifting, that's a warning sign that you're just filling time, not building.

When you know the goal, you can filter out all the stuff that disguises itself as opportunity but is really distraction. Stuff like:

- Small disputes

- Drama with clients or staff

- Side projects

- Things that stroke the ego but don't serve the business

You can easily tell yourself the above things are important, but really, they're just pulling your energy away from what matters. I've been there, caught up in things that feel urgent but aren't important. You will lose days, or even weeks, being pulled into pointless arguments, chasing shiny objects or getting involved in things you've got no business being involved in. It's not productive and it definitely isn't strategic.

Real strategy is saying no to the noise and focusing on the stuff that's going to create long-term value.

One-hour reset

This might feel counter-intuitive, especially when you've got a ton to do, but I swear by the one-hour reset. Every entrepreneur needs to build one into their daily routine, or at the very least do it a few times each week.

A one-hour reset means no distractions, no telly, no background noise and no scrolling on your phone. Just silence and space. One full hour where you do nothing except sit with your own thoughts and ask yourself the real questions:

- What am I working toward?
- Is this aligned with where I want to be?
- Am I moving with purpose or just reacting to noise?

Everyone's overstimulated today. We're permanently glued to our phones, our inboxes and our to-do lists. Even in our downtime, we're drowning in noise – Netflix, TikTok, WhatsApp, the list goes on. There's no mental breathing room. This is why so many founders lose clarity, get burnt out or feel stuck even when they're doing everything right.

If you can't sit in silence with your own mind for an hour, you're not in control, the world is. That one-hour reset is where real strategy forms. Not when you're in the chaos of the day, but when you step back and think clearly, with no noise around you.

If you're juggling multiple ideas or businesses, you must prioritise a regular one-hour reset; otherwise, you'll find yourself working hard but not actually getting anywhere or, just as bad, drifting along aimlessly. The one-hour reset isn't a luxury. It's a non-negotiable habit that keeps your vision sharp and your direction clear.

Set your priorities

One thing that's helped me massively when things get a bit crazy is simply focusing on the single most important thing that needs to get done. Every evening, I write out a list of tasks that must be completed and then go through it and figure out which one is going to make the biggest impact. What's going to push the business forward the most? Then, when I wake up, I already know exactly what needs my focus that day, instead of wasting time figuring out what to do. It doesn't have to be complicated – just a simple to-do list in a notebook or on a whiteboard.

As you might expect from the previous chapter, I use technology to make this process easier. Specifically, I use a diary app called TimeTree. My PA makes sure the most important tasks go straight to the top, because that's where most of my time should go. Everything else? It can wait or be fitted in once I've handled the priority. This makes sure that not a moment is wasted and I don't get perpetually pulled in all directions, getting nothing done.

Of course, businesses are unpredictable. Things change every day, so while I plan ahead, I also adjust as needed. If something urgent comes up, I take a moment to rearrange my priorities accordingly but, even then, I always try to stay aligned with the most important tasks.

If you find that there's an item lingering on your 'to do' list day after day, never getting ticked off, see if you can bump it up the list. Yes, some tasks naturally take weeks or months, but for the smaller ones that can be done in a day, get them done as quickly as possible. The longer you sit on them, the more they pile up and slow you down. Tackle them head-on and move forward.

Time-efficient decision-making

When it comes to deciding on priorities – and here I'm talking about projects, ideas, decisions that need to be made, avenues you're exploring within the business – this requires your judgement and is a skill you will need to develop over time. It's a multi-step process, but the more you practise it, the more natural it will become.

Begin by talking through the idea or decision with people you trust. In my case, this is usually my management team, or close colleagues. If it's a big decision, I might even ask friends and family, though I take outside opinions with a pinch of salt unless they're coming from people who know the ins and outs of what I'm working on. Sometimes, though, just having those conversations and hashing it out can help you spot red flags or opportunities you might've missed.

Next, I'll back-test the idea, asking myself: has something similar worked before? Can I draw comparisons to past situations? Is there a track record, even if it's indirectly related? It requires being honest and applying logic, not being drawn in by hype.

After I've done all of that, it is time for the most powerful part: I sit with it. I'll use my one-hour reset and ask myself:

- What's the best-case scenario?
- What's the worst-case scenario?
- Is this worth the risk?
- What could go wrong?
- What would I do if it did go wrong?
- Does this align with what I'm building?

I try to think five steps ahead because it's not just about what happens if it works, it's about what happens next. If it goes wrong, what's the fallout? If it goes right, does it create more distractions or dependencies? Will it open more value or more complications?

This process, from discussion, to analysis, to sitting with your own thoughts, keeps you grounded. It stops you chasing things that look good on the surface but pull you off track long term. The more intentional you are with your time, the more progress you'll make and the less clean-up you'll have to do later.

Don't be afraid to say no

Where a lot of people go wrong with time management is being too slow to say 'no' to something that will take up too much of their time and is not part of the main business strategy. It's easily done, we get pulled into things because they're something new, it feels exciting and there's the potential to make a quick return or build something fast. Usually, it will become a distraction, not because it's a bad idea on paper, but because it's not aligned with what you're already building. You need to learn to say no.

Saying no is a tough thing to do. This I know well. I've got a couple of stories to share. One where I was sensible enough to say no quickly, and one where I was already invested, but then realised I had made a mistake. In both cases, walking away was tough.

The first example was when my brother talked to me about starting a construction company with him and a couple of other guys. My brother dropped out early on for personal reasons, but I still believed in the idea and really liked the other two guys who were both good, genuine lads, so we went ahead with it.

At the same time, I had other businesses starting to take off, some much quicker than expected. I was stretched and I could feel it. I was in two minds about whether to commit fully to the construction company or not. Part of me didn't want to let my business partners down, not least because we'd built trust, but I had to do something, so I got together with them to hash it out properly. I told them honestly, 'I just haven't got the time to give this what it needs. I'm sorry.' Fair play to them, they completely understood.

The situation just reinforced what I already knew: you've got to be honest with yourself and with others, even when it's uncomfortable. Saying yes when your plate's already full only creates problems later. Being clear, upfront and intentional with your time is the best way to protect your energy, your reputation and your long-term success.

The second time, I'd got further down the line before I said no. In some ways that was more difficult, because I had already spent quite a bit of money. This time, a business partner of mine was on my case trying to get me involved in a recruitment company. He didn't have all the funds himself, so he pushed for me to split the investment with him.

The original proposal was for each of us to invest £20,000 a month over three months. Right away I said, 'No chance.' The setup felt wrong, the people involved weren't the kind I'd usually deal with and it just didn't feel like a smart move. After some negotiation, we got it down to £12,000 over six months. Even then, I still had a bad feeling in my gut, but I let myself get talked into it. I thought I'd give it a go and see what happened in the first month. Deep down though, I knew it wasn't the right call.

Sure enough, as soon as that first payment went out, things started falling apart. The others didn't deliver anything they promised. The company website looked like a five-year-old had built it, their systems were non-existent and it became clear that they were just chasing investment. There was no structure, no direction and nothing that screamed long-term potential.

I pulled out. Yeah, it caused some aggro, because technically I'd agreed to it, but I knew I had to cut the cord before it got worse. That decision saved me a lot more time, stress and money down the line. I should've trusted my gut from day one, but sometimes you let other people's confidence push you into something that deep down, you know isn't right.

It's a hard lesson, but a valuable one: just because something looks like an opportunity, doesn't mean it's the right one for you. Say no early, but even if you do invest time and money, still be prepared to walk away from anything that drains your time.

Delegate

I was talking to a guy recently who moved in near me. He was running a couple of businesses, doing everything himself – a classic one-man-band setup. We were chatting over coffee and he asked me for some advice. He told me the main thing he struggles with is delegation. He's scared to hand over responsibility because he doesn't trust anyone with his clients. I told him straight:

'At some point, you've got to let go. You'll never scale or free yourself up unless you build systems and train people. It's like riding a bike, the only way to learn is to get on and go. Yes, you'll wobble and may even fall a few times, but you get better each time. That's how leadership works.'

If you're running multiple businesses or projects, you simply cannot do everything yourself. Identify what truly needs your attention and delegate the rest so you can focus on the bigger picture.

Earlier I talked about the value in creating a solid team who will call you out when things are off. This culture will come into its own when it comes to time management and delegation. You've got to create an environment where people feel comfortable expressing their thoughts, ideas and opinions and that means telling you when you are over-stretched and when they can and should take something off your hands. They are in the best position to know.

I've also tried to create a culture where people are trusted and given flexibility, which aids delegation. I don't treat people like robots or slaves, which you still see in far too many companies. When people feel trusted and empowered, they take ownership of tasks naturally, you don't need to breathe down their necks or spend time dishing out tasks.

I'm not involved in every single little thing because I simply don't have the time and, more importantly, I shouldn't be knee deep in every detail. That's the whole point of having a team and building a strong leadership layer. My managers handle the day-to-day operations and the rest of the staff, and I stay focused on the bigger picture.

This is why now, day to day, I'm able to spend my time on what actually matters: strategy, growth and steering the ship, rather than drowning in admin.

The benefit of hindsight

I've wasted years focusing on the wrong things, saying yes to too much, getting involved in business partnerships that weren't aligned or trying to force things that weren't meant to happen. Looking back, if I'd just focused – *really* focused – I'd have made more progress, sooner.

If I could go back to when I was first starting out, I'd give myself one simple but powerful rule: don't try to juggle too many things at once. Focus on where you're trying to get to with your first business. That's where your energy needs to go. By prioritising projects and tasks, structuring each day, staying flexible and knowing when to delegate, you can ensure your time is spent where it truly matters: on the things that drive your business forwards.

One of the main reasons I wrote this book is because if I can help someone avoid wasting the years

I wasted, that alone makes it worthwhile. Since time is your most valuable resource, managing it properly is key to staying productive and making real progress. It goes fast, though, so be intentional and spend it in the right places. Don't throw time away just because something seems like it might lead somewhere. Lock in on what you're building and stay there.

11
Coping Under Pressure

There is no point in financial freedom if you're mentally caged. There was a point in my career where the pressure nearly broke me. I was juggling three businesses at once – the training company, the endpoint assessment centre and the sushi restaurant. It was chaos, complete chaos. I don't think I've ever been that stressed before or since. Every day felt like I was firefighting from the second I woke up. There were too many moving parts, too many people depending on me and zero breathing space. I'd be on a work call while trying to handle restaurant staff issues, then immediately switch to training contracts and then compliance headaches, all in the space of minutes. I was spread so thin I could barely think straight.

There were moments I honestly thought I might snap, and I think back to that time a lot. It was a big part of my motivation to write *The Hustle Mindset*. It was the time when I learned that if you want to make it through as an entrepreneur, you have to learn to carry heavy loads without breaking. That means keeping moving, even when it feels like your brain's melting. The minute you stop, that's when it's over. That's when it beats you.

Since that time, I have learned a lot about resilience and I have many strategies I use to keep on track. Back then, though, I got through it with sheer grit and determination. It probably helped that I realised I had no fall back, so I didn't have the luxury of giving up. I reminded myself daily why I started, who I was doing it for and where I was trying to get to. After a while I managed to stop thinking about how overwhelming everything was and just focused on the next thing to do. I didn't allow myself to walk away.

Embrace the mess

We all know someone who talks about their regrets – the business they didn't start, the idea they gave up on or the thing they walked away from too soon. As people get older, you hear it more and more. Almost every time, the difference between them and someone who made it isn't talent or timing; it's resilience. They stuck with it when most people would've folded.

Most fail in the hustle because they're not prepared for the emotional toll this game takes. The pressure is constant – financial, mental and even physical.

There's isolation, self-doubt, imposter syndrome, fear of failure and sometimes fear of success. It's a rollercoaster ride, where one minute you feel like a genius and the next a fraud. That's all normal, but if you don't learn how to ride those highs and lows without losing your focus, you'll crash.

A lot of founders are reluctant to talk about the messier side of running a business because there's this unspoken pressure to paint the perfect picture. Not all founders do this. More people are being open about it now, especially with social media removing the stigma around vulnerability. Yet, there's still a strong tendency to gloss over the chaos and focus on the highlights. Some of it comes down to ego. Let's be honest, when you've put your name to and energy into building something, it's hard to admit when things aren't going smoothly. There's this fear that if you show the cracks, people might think the whole thing is unstable. That kind of transparency can feel risky, especially when you're trying to attract investors, customers or simply respect from your peers. I also think some founders get caught up in the performance of success. They want to appear like they've got everything under control, even when they're barely holding it together. But being real about the struggle doesn't make you weaker; it makes you more relatable, credible and trustworthy.

If anything, the mess is what makes the journey authentic. The more we talk about it, the more we help other founders stop feeling like they're the only ones going through it. The reality is, all businesses are messy. Behind every polished brand there is a team firefighting problems, dealing with unexpected setbacks and figuring stuff out as they go. You can study business at uni, read all the books and sit through endless strategy sessions, but none of that prepares you for the chaos of the real thing. Those are the moments that really test you, but they also shape you. When you don't give up and a year later, you're back on your feet, stronger and smarter – that's when you realise what you're made of.

You'll be surprised by what you're capable of achieving if you're genuinely resilient and you're willing to put your mind to it. Over the years, my view on resilience has shifted from thinking it was just about 'toughing it out' to something deeper. Now I see it as a mindset, a skill and a habit. You can learn to be more resilient, which is why I'm sharing what I now know.

Resilience is one of the most important traits in business, hands down. Without resilience, nothing else matters. You could have the best idea, the best team and the best setup, but if you crumble the first time things don't go your way, you won't make it.

Dealing with the pressure and uncertainty

It's hard to describe unless you've actually lived it, but setting up and running a business is a mental drain like no other. It's probably one of the loneliest places you can be, because, deep down, you know no one's coming to save you. No one's going to jump in and take the weight off your shoulders and most people, even those closest to you, won't fully understand what you're going through.

It wears you down physically, too. You'll feel exhausted all the time, stop sleeping properly and your body will be (just about) running on adrenaline and fumes. It's like being underwater, trying to breathe while juggling with one hand.

Before long, you'll start to feel like you're slipping out of control and the worst part is, you won't know where the bottom is. All you can do is to hope it ends in a way that doesn't wreck everything and that you come out of it still standing and able to carry on. It's a scary place to be, stuck in that unknown, with no idea what the next few weeks or months are going to bring and praying all your bets pay off.

The realisation that you are succumbing to the pressure doesn't come all at once. It builds up as you face issue after issue – someone on the team dropping the ball, customers slipping through the cracks, money getting mismanaged or communication breaking down. For me, the scenario I described at the beginning of the chapter was less of a lightbulb moment and more of a hard lesson learned over time. The more you grow, the more you realise that the hustle mindset can only take you so far. You need strategies to prop you up and keep you on track when things get tough.

It's probably not what you want to hear, but the feelings of being out of control may never fully go away, whatever strategies you adopt. That constant nagging sensation because you are juggling too much, spinning too many plates and keeping things just about together is part and parcel of building your own thing. There's no magic formula or easy way out of it, because when you're doing something meaningful, it's always going to come with pressure.

What I can tell you from experience, though, is that it does get easier to manage. While the uncertainty never fully goes away, your relationship with it can change. You can learn to ride the wave without drowning and stay calm in the chaos. To do this, you need to take control of your time, energy, team and health – both mental and physical. Building strong systems and a solid team are invaluable steps in managing pressure and making sure you survive without burning out. You also need to focus on you. Let's look now at how to keep your mental and physical health a priority, even when in the midst of building your business.

Mental resilience

One of the biggest misconceptions about mental 'toughness' in entrepreneurship is that it means being emotionless, robotic or never struggling. People think if you're mentally tough that nothing fazes you, you're always confident and you never doubt yourself. That's nonsense. Real mental toughness is the ability to keep showing up even when everything feels like it's falling apart. It's not about feeling invincible.

A lot of people get into entrepreneurship thinking they're mentally strong because they're super motivated at the start. They think they've got the grit because they can pull an all-nighter or give 110% when they're fired up. True mental toughness kicks in after the hype fades. When the excitement's gone, your bank balance is low, your team's losing belief and the wins are few and far between – that's when you find out if you're really built for this.

Control your thoughts

For me, the key to mental resilience is learning to control your thoughts. It's crucial to manage your mind so that it doesn't run wild. This means checking your self-talk, grounding yourself daily and not letting temporary hiccups convince you the whole ship is sinking. When things get heavy, I zoom out and actively remind myself that these are just bad moments. If you let panic guide your decisions, they'll always turn out badly.

As a step-by-step process, taking control of your thoughts when you hit a setback or things get too much, goes something like this:

1. **Take a step back:** First, stop everything and just give yourself space. When you hit a setback, the natural reaction is to panic, overthink or to go straight into 'fix it' mode. But if you act too fast, you'll usually be acting out of emotion, not logic – that's how bad decisions happen. Give yourself

time alone to think – switch off the noise, remove the distractions and properly sit with the issue. Process the setback before reacting to it, otherwise, your ego gets involved, fear kicks in or worse, you start blaming other people. That doesn't move you forward. First get calm, then get clear.

2. **Simplify:** When everything feels out of control, simplify. Break it down and focus on one priority at a time rather than trying to solve twenty problems at once. Solve the problem in front of you, then move on to the next.

3. **Think strategically:** With each issue, ask yourself: *What's the new play? How do I pivot? How do I use this loss to create a better outcome?* This is the time to reach out to the people you trust. You're not asking them to fix it for you, but it's good to get outside perspective from people you respect, who've been in the trenches with you. Remember, not everyone's opinion matters, only the ones who've got real skin in the game.

4. **Execute:** You then need to get back in motion, because that's how you turn a loss into a win. If something doesn't look like it is going the way you want it to, have the tough conversations you need to have straight away. Don't hang around, crossing your fingers and hoping it will improve. There is a high probability it won't. Things will go wrong, but that could be beyond your control; it's how you deal with them that counts.

This four-step process will help you to reframe setbacks, which is one of the most powerful things you can do as a business owner. Setbacks are inevitable. Whether they define you is a choice. When it comes to day-to-day stresses and strains, I find it helps to write things down as I go along. Stress multiplies when it's trapped in your mind, and an endless list of things to do clouds your thoughts. The moment you externalise it, it loses some of its power.

Pressure is the price of being an entrepreneur. If you expect it to be easy, you'll be crushed, but if you accept that stress is part of the journey and learn to carry it, it makes you sharper.

Control your physical state

Your physical health is just as important as your mental health, and your physiology affects your decisions. I didn't realise how true this was until I started training consistently, using the sauna and ice baths, and even simple things like deep breathing. When your body is calm, your brain can think clearly.

When you're building businesses and going a hundred miles an hour, your health can end up taking a backseat. You're running around, constantly stressed, eating crap on the go, maybe drinking more than usual and staying up late. This all catches up with you. When things were going wrong for me, I'd be working late, grabbing a takeaway, maybe opening a bottle of wine while replying to emails and then waking up feeling like absolute shit. At the time, I was also dealing with issues related to my immune system, something I had to take medication for, and I knew I couldn't carry on the way I was. That's when I came across hyperbaric oxygen therapy. I looked into it and saw that it wasn't just good for your immune system, but also helped with inflammation, stress, brain fog and recovery, so I gave it a go. I started noticing the benefits pretty quickly. My energy improved, my thinking became sharper and I was sleeping better. It gave me the mental edge I didn't realise I was missing.

Push your limits

Once I recognised how important my physical wellbeing was, I was all in. That is the type of person I am. That's how I got into ice baths.

When I sit in that freezing water, I get a real sense of achievement. It makes me feel lighter somehow. I found out about them after watching a few podcasts with Wim Hoff, aka 'the Ice Man'. Scientific studies have shown that it trains your brain to down-regulate stress and improves tolerance to discomfort, because when you constantly do something you don't want to do, it makes you more inclined to do other things you don't want to do.[6] It's the same logic behind why,

---

[6] A Yankouskaya, R Williamson, C Stacey, JJ Totman and H Massey, 'Short-term head-out whole-body cold-water immersion facilitates positive affect and increases interaction between large-scale brain networks', *Biology*, 12/2 (2023), https://pmc.ncbi.nlm.nih.gov/articles/PMC9953392, accessed 13 January 2026

COPING UNDER PRESSURE

if you fear something, you should do it. If you don't, you will keep procrastinating and become lazy. If you are not pushing your body and mind to the limits, you're never going to overcome the challenges you face.

Try it. You'll never know until you do. You don't have to spend a fortune. I started with a cheap version, just a black box you put ice cubes in, then I eventually invested in a proper ice bath. To begin with, I set it at 10 degrees but I managed to get it down to 3, its lowest setting. I confess, I did overdo it, taking ice baths twice a day every day of the week, which I wouldn't recommend. I started feeling very tired and later found out this was because I was putting my body under a massive amount of stress, as it was desperately trying to warm up from inside, too frequently. So don't do it every day, kids. Three or four times a week, max, is fine.

Lately, I've got into saunas, too, which are great for muscle relaxation and stress reduction. I like the fact that they detoxify the body, because you literally sweat out the crap, but most of all, being in there is a guaranteed moment of silence in a chaotic day.

I don't do ice baths and saunas because they sound cool, but because they genuinely reset me. They give me a natural dopamine hit and keep me level. The better you feel, the better the decisions you make and the more control you have over your life and business. To perform at a high level in business, you need to be dialled-in both mentally and physically. You can't separate the two. If your body's run down, your mind suffers and when your mind suffers, so does your decision making. In business, that can cost you money, time and relationships.

For me, this stuff is as important as checking emails or closing deals. If your brain's foggy, your body's sluggish and your stress levels are through the roof, you're not going to perform. You're going to procrastinate, make poor choices and eventually burn out. Since I made these things part of my weekly routine, I've been more productive, more focused and sharper in every area of business.

Don't self-sabotage

A few years ago, if you'd asked me how I switch off, I probably would've said, 'Rest? That's what the afterparty's for.' Back then, weekends were raves, parties and nights out with mates – a full switch-off, but not a healthy one. These days, things are different. With so much going on during the week – the operations of multiple businesses, calls, meetings, Zooms and managing teams – I always tell myself that I'll use the weekend to reset and rewind. I wouldn't say I ever manage to switch off completely, though. Nine times out of ten, I still end up researching something, jotting down ideas or checking in on a few bits. That's just how my brain's wired now; I'm always thinking about growth, systems and how to get to that next level. However much I try to switch off, it never fully works.

With a lifestyle like this, it can be tempting to fast-track the unwind. I've been there. I've done the self-sabotage. I've seen plenty of other founders do it too. You go out all the time, drink too much, eat like shit, live off adrenaline and caffeine, and then wonder why your mind is a mess. But if you flip that around and start taking care of yourself, things get clearer. Some founders never make this link, and it can easily end badly.

Choose your friends wisely

Let me tell you about Adam. He ran a hugely successful business bringing home six figures a year, more money than he ever thought he'd make. But there was a problem: he couldn't stop self-sabotaging.

Outside of work, Adam still spent most of his time with the same group of mates he'd grown up with. In itself, this isn't an issue, as staying grounded is important. But these guys weren't just a group of old friends. They were reckless – drinking, taking drugs and staying out all night, three or four times a week. Adam was caught in the middle, trying to run a company while also maintaining a lifestyle that no longer fitted him. A lot of it was because he couldn't let go of the people who were holding him back, but I think it was also a subconscious way of relieving some of the pressure.

For me, it's simple: stay away from people who drag you into a lifestyle that will stop you achieving your business goals. That's probably been the biggest shift I've made over the years. You become who you spend time with – that's not just a saying, that's real. If you hang around with people who are always on it, partying every weekend and living for the now, you'll get sucked into that, despite any good intentions. If you're under pressure and looking for a relief from the relentless grind, it is even easier to get pulled off course by this kind of behaviour.

It can be hard to cut certain people off – mates you've known for years, maybe even family. But if they're encouraging you to forget your goals, draining your energy or clinging to the old version of you and trying to stop you changing, you've got to distance yourself. That doesn't mean you hate them. It just means you're choosing your future over your past.

Not everyone can do it. When I pulled Adam aside and said, 'Mate, you need to step away from this,' he nodded and admitted that he knew that his friends were dragging him down. But he didn't step away. It wasn't just that the pull of loyalty was too strong; they seemed to give him the escape he craved.

So, what happened? His business collapsed. The late nights turned into missed meetings. The partying blurred into his professional life and clients lost faith in him. By the time he realised he was destroying his business, it was too late.

Here's the brutal truth: the path you're on now is different. You don't live a 'normal' life anymore. You've chosen something harder, something riskier, but also something that can bring you success beyond what most people even dream about. Not everyone around you will understand this or support you. Some people may even actively try to pull you back down – usually at the point when you're at your most vulnerable because of the pressure you're under. Don't let them.

If you don't control your environment, your environment will control you. My best advice is to make an active resolution to stay healthy and to moderate the bad stuff. I'm not saying I'm perfect. I'm still human and still have the odd blowout here and there. I won't pretend I don't. The difference is that now I feel the after-effects more. One big night, a few drinks, some crap food and I wake up the next day feeling like I've been hit by a bus. The fog, low energy and stress levels kill my momentum. When you're running a business and making big decisions daily, that kind of setback costs you – physically, mentally and financially. If you're regularly finding yourself in this position, follow the advice I set out in the previous sections because when your body is in a good place, your mind follows. If you feel strong, well-rested and properly fuelled, you won't want to self-sabotage. You'll naturally be more focused, driven and locked in. Discipline is easier when your energy's high.

Self-sabotage doesn't happen because you're weak. It happens because you're not protecting your inputs, whether that's your people, habits or headspace, because these are what keep you on course.

Failure is a mindset

In business, things will go wrong. Very wrong. In fact, if they don't, you're not trying hard enough. It doesn't feel good to fail. Far from it. Sometimes, when things have gone badly, I have been left physically shaking with the stress of it. I've even felt stressed in my sleep. There's nothing worse than feeling that your world has ended – or is about to. When it happens, though, I remind myself that it's just a step on the road and I need to deal with it as what it is.

Endurance is more important than intensity. Anyone can hustle hard for a day or a week, but can you stay in the game? When you're overloaded and under pressure, can you still show up like it matters? That's the real test. Most people don't fail because they're not smart enough; they fail because they can't hold their nerve when it gets rough.

There will be moments when it just feels too much and your only wish is to walk away from it all. Those moments come more often than people think, especially when you're in deep, juggling multiple things and nothing seems to be going right. It's not just me; every serious entrepreneur I've ever spoken to has had those days. You question everything and sometimes you sit there thinking, *What the hell am I doing this for?*

Thinking about quitting and actually walking away are two completely different things. Once you've been on this ride for a while, built things from scratch, made your own decisions and controlled your own money, time and indeed life, going back to working for someone else just isn't an option. The idea of slotting back into a nine-to-five, clocking in and out, asking someone for permission to take time off – that, to me, would feel like settling. It would be like getting back into a cage I've worked hard to escape.

To get through it all, I have learned to view failure in a different way. In my head, I *can't* fail. I genuinely don't see it as an option. I've got too much on the line and too many people depending on me. That weight of responsibility, of knowing other people's livelihoods are tied to your decisions, changes everything. It keeps you going when others would give up.

Yes, there have been times when I have lost everything and watched something I've built collapse. That kind of loss hits hard and takes the wind out of you, but I have never once called it 'failure'. To me, failing isn't losing everything – it's not getting back up. If you're still moving, learning and building something out of the ashes of a crisis, you haven't failed, you've just taken a hit.

Failure is a mindset. This is about how you label the experience of things falling apart. If you see it as the end, it becomes the end. If, however, you see it as a lesson, it becomes fuel. That's how I've always looked at it and I would urge you to do the same. You won't just bounce back from setbacks, you'll come back smarter, sharper and more committed than ever. People who make it in business don't avoid failure; they just don't attach their whole being to it. Instead, they learn, adapt and push forward.

THE HUSTLE MINDSET

Once you start this journey, you're in it. There's no going back, and you probably won't want to. Even when it's tough, there's something about building your own thing that keeps you coming back for more. It's not for everyone, but if you're wired like this, you'll get it.

Mental toughness and resilience in the face of failure isn't loud. It's quiet, consistent and often invisible. It's the decision to keep building when no one's watching and no one believes in you. That's the real hustle mindset.

12
When People Try To Hustle Your Hustle

When you start making moves, you'll notice a strange shift: people who were nowhere to be seen in the hard times suddenly want to 'get involved' the moment things look promising. It starts with flattery: 'You're doing bits!' Then come the DMs, the catch-up calls and the vague business ideas they want to hear your opinion on. Next, they'll tell you their 'real dream' is to collaborate with you, or partner on something so you can build a business together. Don't be won over by the charm offensive – look closely, are they offering any real value? Often, what they really want is to jump on your momentum.

These people don't want to carry weight and do anything useful. They want to ride your success and make it theirs. This is one of the biggest traps you'll face as a business builder: people trying to hustle on your hustle. I call them cling-ons.

Beware cling-ons

Cling-ons aren't always easy to spot at first. Some are charming, many are convincing and a few might genuinely seem like they are being helpful. When you cut through the surface, though, you'll see the signs that they have a different agenda entirely.

Awkwardly, a cling-on will often be a good friend and someone you've known for a while. This is another reason to keep a clear line between friendship and business. Mixing the two rarely ends well. I honestly can't name a single time when doing business with a friend, on equal footing, ended in anything but tension, resentment or awkward conversations down the line. The dynamic changes. What starts off as 'just helping out' quickly becomes entitlement, blurred responsibilities and emotional baggage tied to decisions that should stay strictly professional. The hard truth is that when friends want to get involved, what this often means is they want to skip the queue. They want in on the upside without going through the same process as everyone else.

When acquaintances pop up out of nowhere after seeing your wins, it's usually opportunistic. It's important to see this for what it is and react accordingly. If someone wasn't with you when you were grinding, they shouldn't get an unearned seat when things start looking shiny. I'll always be respectful, but I don't hand out positions, titles or equity as favours. That's not how you build something that lasts.

I noticed this phenomenon pretty early on, around the time I was starting my third business. When it happened, I didn't want to recognise it for what it was. I've always tried to see the best in people and definitely struggled with people-pleasing in the early days. To be fair to myself, when you're new to running a business, it's unknown territory. You're stepping into a completely different world. Suddenly, you're the one calling the shots, and that can mess with your head a bit. You want people to like you and you want to be fair. You don't want to come across as too harsh, cold or corporate. Saying no to people you know, especially friends, or someone you've got a relationship with, can feel awkward. Maybe I was still a bit naïve, too, assuming without question that if someone smiled at me, or showed up when things were going well, they had my back. What I have learned since is that you never understand what people are truly like until money, opportunity or status are involved. Trying to please everyone is the fastest way to burn yourself out and stall your momentum.

It wasn't a single moment that made me wake up to this important lesson; it was something that revealed itself over time. I noticed a pattern: when things were good, business was booming, the money was rolling in and clients lined up, people were everywhere, all over me, all the time. The phone was always ringing, messages were flying in and people I didn't even know that well were offering help left and right. Strangely, though, when things dipped or got tough, those same people vanished. Crickets. There was no support, the regular check-ins stopped – just silence. That's when I clocked what was really going on.

Not everyone is malicious in doing this. Some cling-ons don't even realise they're doing it. They just think that's how the game works – you get in early, hang around and it'll somehow pay off. But some very clearly know what they are doing. They're calculating. They see you building something and think, *If I stick close enough, I'll get a slice without doing the graft.* They are obvious opportunists. Oddly, though, I'd say the people who don't realise they're freeloading are almost more dangerous. They are less easy to spot, and you might not be as on your guard as you need to be.

What people like this will never understand is, there's a massive difference between being *around* the hustle and being *in* it. Just being near the fire doesn't mean that you lit it. When you let someone like this linger in your business or your circle, it costs you energy, speed and clarity. Worst of all, it can make you second-guess yourself. You'll find that you're constantly asking yourself, *Am I being too harsh? Should I give them another chance?* You'll kid yourself that they'll step up eventually, but deep down, you already know that they won't. If someone wanted to add value, they'd be doing it. Likewise, if they wanted to be a real part of your journey, you wouldn't have to convince them or chase them. Their commitment would shine through.

Spotting the red flags

I've thought about this a lot, imagining that if I understood them better, I'd be better at resisting the overtures of a cling-on. As far as I can tell, their main motivations are:

- Lack of drive – they're lazy and looking for the path of least resistance
- Lack of confidence – they're afraid to start something themselves, so they look for someone who already has
- Fear of missing out – they see your momentum and want in, without any of the risk
- Entitlement – they think they deserve a seat at the table just because they know you

Nowadays, whenever anyone tells me they want to 'collaborate' or 'partner' with me, the first thing I look at is their track record. By this I mean not just what they say they've done – because cling-ons are masters at talking the talk – I want to know what they've actually built, delivered or grown. Talk is cheap, especially in business. Anyone can dress up their LinkedIn and talk big, but results don't lie. I want to know: What have they *done*? What have they failed at and bounced back from? What have they built for themselves, not been handed?

I also look carefully at the value they're offering and, more importantly, why they think they can offer it. If someone wants to collaborate, I ask them what skill set they're bringing and why they are the right person for this project at this moment.

Now that I'm more experienced, I don't let people approach me for partnerships in the way that I used to. Today I build with intention and pick who I want to work with before the idea even gets moving. I've spent years gathering a solid network around me, so when I've got something new on the table, I already know who's trustworthy, who delivers and who's aligned with the vision. I've long stopped rolling the dice and instead I hand-pick people to work with based on history, not hype. This is a learned skill, but below is a list of red flags based on my years of experience. If you think you are attracting the attention of cling-ons, use it to assess if someone is right for you and your project, or just trying to steal your hustle. I advise vigilance here – if they show even one of these red flags, you need to be on your guard:

- **Over eagerness:** If someone is pushing too hard to collaborate, even before they have heard the full plan, this shows it's all about them, not the mission.

- **They offer ideas not action:** They're full of visions and suggestions, but never take ownership. They want to be on the call, in the meeting and at the table, but they never send the follow-up email, chase the lead or write the proposal. They talk around the work, not through it.

- **They leverage proximity, not productivity:** Their whole game is to be close to the action. They try to be seen near you, involved with you and associated with your brand. Whenever possible, they connect your name with theirs, even if they haven't contributed. They appear to think that being near the hustle is the same as building it.

- **They ask for opportunities before earning them:** They'll try to get a piece of the pie without providing any of the ingredients. That could be a cut of the company, a job title or a percentage of future deals. Whatever it is, they want in early without proving anything. They say, 'Let's do this together', but what they mean is, 'Let me in on what you've already started'.

- **They drain energy:** This one you'll feel. You'll be spending more time explaining, managing or motivating them than you do focusing on the actual business. They bring drama, confusion or chaos instead of clarity and execution. They are emotional liabilities, not business assets.

- **They disappear when it's time to deliver:** They are present for the brainstorm, but absent for the deadline. They've always got an excuse and a reason to not follow through, whether it's timing, personal stuff, confusion or bad luck. Meanwhile, you're left picking up the slack. Again.

At this level, collaboration isn't just about energy, it's about alignment. You don't need yes-men (or women) or hype merchants. You need people who show up when things are heavy and still execute.

> **Hustle mindset tip for collaborating**
>
> The people who are right for your project usually don't need to sell themselves to you. Their work speaks for them.

The cost of keeping the peace

Giving in to cling-ons costs more than just your sanity. When someone is giving it all that and switches on the full-on charm offensive, it is really difficult to turn away. We're all vulnerable to a bit of flattery, especially if we are stressed and exhausted by the daily grind. In the early days, I said yes to people out of guilt, pressure or just because I was caught up in the moment. The biggest lesson I've learned from that is that once you say yes, it's hard to go back. You can't un-ring that bell.

One of the clearest examples was when I agreed to a fifty-fifty split on a business. In the moment, it felt right and the guy involved had been badgering me for ages and telling me I was the only person in the world with the drive and know-how to bring that company to life. There was excitement, momentum and ideas flowing all over the place. Looking back, though, it made no sense. I was bringing the connections, the experience, the strategy and the actual infrastructure to make it work, and all he was bringing was enthusiasm. If I had seen through all the praise and flattery, I'd have recognised that he had no real track record or any skin in the game. Yet, because I was just starting out and wanted to avoid awkwardness by keeping the vibe positive, I agreed to the split.

As I quickly learned, it was a big mistake. It was a completely uneven match, and giving him 50% of the shares in the business was absurd. It was a painful lesson: just because someone thinks they're entitled to 50% of something, it doesn't mean that it's the right thing to do. Trying to change that further down the line, even if a reduced stake is clearly justified, is nearly impossible. When the business starts gaining traction and the imbalance between who is doing what or has the most valuable skills becomes obvious, they're never going to turn around and say, 'Yeah, fair enough, you deserve more, let's adjust the split.' It just doesn't happen. People rarely, if ever, give up power or equity willingly, especially when they didn't earn it in the first place. When you say yes, you create an expectation and trying to walk that back always leads to resentment and conflict.

I've made this mistake more than once and it always comes from the same place: trying to keep the peace, wanting to be seen as fair and to move quickly. But it's not fair. Making decisions and acting without logic is just bad business. These days, I don't make decisions based on hype or feelings. I get clear on what value is being added, and by whom, before I shake hands.

How to protect your hustle

Every time you say yes to something that doesn't align with your mission, you're effectively saying no to something that does. These days, I say no a lot, especially to things that come from outside my circle, my team or my core business. I've built a strong filter for where I will put my time, energy and attention. If it doesn't add value or align with the bigger picture, I don't entertain it. Cling-ons can flatter me all they like, I ain't buying.

The funny thing is, since I started saying no more often, everything's become easier. I have fewer distractions, make better decisions and execute what needs to be done more smoothly. People might not like it at first, but they respect it; the ones who don't probably had their own agenda anyway.

These things get easier with experience, but that takes time. As I've already been through it and learned the lessons, here's my approach to protecting your hustle and staying sharp:

1. **Qualify everyone:** If someone wants in, ask them straight out what they are bringing to the table. If the question makes them uncomfortable, you've got your answer.

2. **Set boundaries early:** Don't give away roles, responsibilities or equity based on friendship or good vibes. Make people earn their place.

3. **Trust patterns, not potential:** If someone keeps falling short even before you've agreed to go into business with them, believe their behaviour, not their excuses. People show you who they are through what they do.

4. **Keep your circle tight and intentional:** The right people will make things easier, faster and clearer. The wrong people will slow you down, stress you out and hold you back. Don't believe the flattery and always listen to your gut feelings.

Ultimately, everyone wants to be part of something successful, but very few want to do what it takes to get there. If you're the one driving the vision, doing the work and taking the risks, you've earned the right to protect your progress. You don't owe anyone access just because they know your name or shared an idea. You're building something real and no one deserves to just come along for the ride.

13
Investing In Other Businesses

In recent years, I've adopted an entirely new approach to doing business, one that has transformed how I operate as an entrepreneur. Instead of starting every business from scratch, I invest in other people's businesses. I don't need to be an expert in that sector; I find people who are specialists in their field and bring my own expertise to the table, whether that's advising on strategy, scaling, funding or operations. In return, I take a slice of the business.

This is where so many entrepreneurs go wrong. They're obsessed with owning the whole thing. They want full control and don't want to share the pie. The reality is that a small slice of something huge is worth far more than full ownership of something small. I'd rather have 20% of a multimillion-pound company than own 100% of a small, struggling one.

Shared success

Take some of the biggest success stories in business, most of those companies aren't owned by one person. Jeff Bezos didn't build Amazon alone. Elon Musk didn't create Tesla by himself. They partnered with the right people, secured good investments and leveraged expertise beyond their own.

The reason this strategy works so well is simple: there are only so many hours in a day. If you're trying to run multiple businesses by yourself, you will burn out. If you collaborate, your reach multiplies. You're no longer limited by what you alone can achieve; you'll have a team of specialists working alongside you, all firing guns in different directions. It's the difference between having a whole grape to yourself or taking a juicy slice of a massive watermelon. The better choice is obvious.

What I really like about my new strategy of investing in businesses is that it allows me to keep doing everything else I do. The income I earn from these ventures supports my lifestyle, covers my wage and, most importantly, lets me take bigger risks on the businesses I am starting up myself. Without that, some of the moves I make wouldn't be possible.

Take one of my current projects: a recruitment company I co-founded with Alicia, a friend of mine who's been working in investment banking recruitment. She was earning £45k a year in her role, but when we got chatting, I learned that placing someone in her field of work can bring into the recruitment

INVESTING IN OTHER BUSINESSES

firm a commission of 20–25% on a £400k salary. You only need a few placements a year to turn that into a serious business. She was unhappy in her job, so I said, 'Why don't we build something for ourselves?' The setup cost me maybe £5k, just for the website, some contracts and the basic infrastructure. It was low risk, with high potential – the perfect proposition. We split the equity: I own 35%, my business partner Poppy owns 15% and Alicia holds 50%. Poppy's handling contracts and admin, I provided the funds and structure and Alicia runs it.

This is what I love: low-touch investments where I can bring experience, not daily involvement. Sometimes I spot an opportunity and then find someone I trust to run it. Other times, people come to me. Either way, I've built a system where I can invest smartly, get a share of the upside and leave the day-to-day to the right people. If I've got a percentage in several different businesses, none of which I have to run, it becomes multiple streams of passive income. If they bring in even £1,000 a month each, it all adds up to a decent sum. That's the play.

Having got this far in the book, you'll know I don't jump at every opportunity. Over the years I've had so many people pitch me ideas – 'We're starting this,' 'Invest in that' – but most of it is noise. I've learned to say no unless I really know the person, have seen their work ethic and believe in the idea. I'm also very careful about the amount of money I commit. A £5k setup cost for a recruitment business? That's low risk. If, on the other hand, a potential investment is going to swallow £12k a month for the foreseeable future, well, that's just too great a risk. Most importantly, I am exceptionally careful with my due diligence. The investment strategy works like a dream, but only when the business is good. When it isn't and something is overlooked? It can be a nightmare.

Finding good investments

Having been burnt a few times over the years, my number one filter when weighing up new investments is the person behind the business. This is based on a specific personal experience.

Early on in the pandemic, while stuck at home recovering from a bout of COVID, I was searching online for anything that might help my dog, who was having constant stomach issues. Somewhere in the depths of Google, I stumbled across a natural compound packed with minerals sold as a supplement for dogs. Intriguingly, the exact same formula was sold for humans, just packaged differently. You just need to add a few drops in water, or mix it in with food. It's simple, natural and powerful.

My research led me to Nikki, the woman behind the product. She was an older lady, kind-hearted but clearly set in her ways. We got talking, first about dogs and then the conversation drifted to business. Nikki's operation was modest, to say the least. She was selling maybe ten bottles of the natural compound a month. She was doing no marketing, had no growth strategy and was relying on a quiet trickle of sales to loyal customers. Out of nowhere, she floated the idea: would I be interested in investing in her company?

It sounded simple enough. The product had potential. She proposed I take 40% of the business in exchange for a £25k investment, with her retaining 60%. Initially, it seemed fair – until I asked for the financials. That's when the red flags started waving. The deeper I dug, the more obvious it became that the business wasn't profitable. In fact, it was barely keeping its head above water. Nikki had sunk money into bulk stock that just sat there, slowly ticking towards the end of its two-year shelf-life expiry date. What was pitched to me as a profitable little venture was, in reality, a money pit. But I was intrigued enough not to want to walk away completely. Instead, I pushed back a little, telling Nikki that I would take 60% not 40%, because the business was running at a loss.

She wasn't having it. Nikki dug in her heels, insisting she wouldn't budge from her controlling share. 'It's my business,' she said. 'I want to stay in charge.' I tried reasoning with her, emphasising that I'd be doing the marketing – I had access to influencers and could leverage my dog-focused Instagram page – and would also be handling distribution, fulfilment, all of it. No dice. She couldn't seem to get her head around the fact that you can't grow a business unless there's the cashflow to market it. It's like having a Ferrari with no engine. It isn't going anywhere.

Eventually, I walked away, telling her that I could easily set this up myself from scratch for less money. I'd given her every chance to partner, but she declined. Life got busy and I didn't have the bandwidth to start the business alone, so I shelved the idea. Even so, I always had the feeling that the natural compound for dogs had potential. It wasn't a get-rich-quick idea, but it had the makings of a solid, steady little e-commerce business – nothing flashy, but something dependable.

Fast forward a while, and I brought the idea up to Poppy, who is creative, organised and was looking for a new project. She jumped at it. The deal we agreed was simple: I'd fund it and she'd run the day-to-day operation. Poppy ran with it. We designed the brand, built the website, created the packaging – all the nuts and bolts that Nikki had never tackled. Meanwhile, I sourced the supplier, found a fulfilment centre and handled the operational backend. We opted for a Fulfilment by Amazon (FBA) model where stock would be shipped directly from our supplier in Canada to the warehouse in Essex and orders would be dispatched automatically. We didn't have to touch a thing.

Our new brand, Rejuvic, launched with human drops, dog drops and sachets, with plans for skin creams and more health products down the line. What started as a random search for a dog supplement during COVID has become a fully-fledged side business. It's not going to make either of us rich overnight, but it's clean, scalable and runs in the background.

The lesson here is that buying an existing business might seem like a shortcut, and it can be – but you must ask the hard questions and you need to know who you are getting into business with. If the deal starts feeling lopsided, you need to trust your gut. Sometimes, walking away is the smartest business move you can make.

So, how do you decide who you'll be able to work with when buying into an existing business? For me, it comes down to three things:

1. **They are an expert in their field:** I look for someone who lives and breathes what they do. They have deep knowledge, a proven track record and a real passion for the business.

2. **They need help scaling:** Just because someone is an expert, doesn't mean they know how to grow a business. That's where I come in. I bring the systems, strategies and funding to take it to the next level.

3. **They have the right mindset:** This is crucial. I don't work with people who just want a quick cash grab. I work with those who are committed, hardworking and willing to do what it takes to win.

When you get this balance right, everyone wins. They get a business partner who helps them scale faster and more efficiently, and you get to be part of something far bigger than you could build alone.

Good business or great business?

Let's assume that all the potential investments you are looking at pass the 'good partnership' test. In other words, the people involved meet the above three criteria. How do you decide if their business is going to be a great investment, or a bit of a dud? You'll come across plenty of businesses that are profitable, well-positioned in their markets and even showing some year-on-year growth. On the surface, they'll seem solid. Dig a little deeper though, and the differences between a good investment and a *great* one become clear.

A good business makes consistent, reliable profit. That's no small achievement. A *great* business not only makes profit, but does so in a way that's scalable. The systems are in place, or are easy to implement, so that revenue can grow without the overheads ballooning alongside it. You're not just buying what the business is now; you're buying into what it can *become*, with a bit of momentum behind it.

That momentum is everything. Timing also plays a huge role. Great investments are often those that are either perfectly positioned to ride an upward wave, or poised to shake up a stagnant market. A good investment might be ticking along at a steady pace, but a great one? It feels like it's about to take off. That sense of upwards trajectory makes all the difference, especially if you're stepping in early.

Then there's the operational side. In great businesses, the day-to-day runs like a machine. Sales, marketing, customer service – everything hums along, and you can see how it could be scaled up. Processes are consistent, people are in the right roles and you're not reliant on one person being there twenty-four-seven. Compare that to a good business, where a lot might still be driven by the founder's hustle or ad-hoc systems. It works, but it's fragile. If you pull back the curtain and see chaos, that's a red flag.

The owner's mindset is another big indicator. Good businesses are usually run by someone competent and passionate. Great businesses are led by people with *vision*. They've built something with a clear destination in mind, whether that's scale, sale or market dominance. When someone's thinking long term and strategically from day one, the business reflects that. It's cleaner, more focused and easier to step into as an investor.

Sometimes, the best opportunities aren't the flashiest. They're the ones where you can see the gap. Maybe the marketing's weak, the pricing's a bit off or they haven't entered adjacent markets that are clearly within reach. A great business leaves room for you to add value. That's the sweet spot: something solid, but not yet at its full potential. You know what to tweak, and you know the impact it will have.

Lastly, consider risk versus reward. Every investment carries risk; that's part of the game. But in a truly great deal, the upside should far outweigh the downside. You're not gambling. Even if it doesn't explode into something huge, the floor is still solid. Worst-case scenario, you've got something that holds value. Best-case? You're looking at a multiple return.

When you've looked at enough deals, you start to get a feel for what makes a great prospect. Two businesses might look similar on paper, but only one of them will have real legs. You'll see it in the way they're run, their ability to grow without breaking and by how little they depend on the founder being in the trenches every day.

Investment due diligence

When I'm looking at whether to invest in a business, there are a few key things I always evaluate; the decision is never based on just one factor. One of the priorities, though, is the financials. I always start by looking at the numbers. Are the accounts clean? Is the business profitable, or at least trending in the right direction? Are there any signs of cash flow issues or poor financial management? You can learn a lot about how a business is run by how they keep their books.

Follow the money

There are a few elements that are absolutely non-negotiable when it comes to financials. If I'm going to invest in a business, I need to see the full picture, not just the highlight reel. That means company accounts, bank statements, cash flow projections, profit and loss statements – the lot. I want to see exactly how money comes in and how it goes out. If there is any caginess about handing over financial information, that's usually all I need to know. Transparency is key. If I'm putting money in, I need to know what I'm walking into, not just what they want me to see.

I'll always look closely at the wage bill. How much is being spent on staff, and is that money being spent wisely? Sometimes, I'll see that a business is paying way too much for roles that don't drive growth. Worse still, I'll see directors pulling big wages while the company is barely profitable.

I also want to look at things like aged debtors and creditors. How quickly is this business getting paid and how long are they taking to pay others? This is a real indication about whether they are managing cash properly, or relying on credit to survive. If their cash flow is all over the place, it doesn't matter how much revenue they're bringing in, the business isn't sustainable.

Margins are a big one, too. A company might be turning over millions, but if their profit margins are razor thin, one price increase or a market shift could wipe them out. I want to see healthy margins, consistent revenue and signs of smart financial management.

Another thing to look at is *where* the money's being spent. Are they reinvesting in growth, or are they just spending for the sake of it? Some companies get caught up in the hype, paying for flashy offices, unnecessary software and overpriced consultants. Lean, efficient spending shows they understand what moves the needle.

All of this is not just about checking numbers; it's about seeing if the patterns make sense and making sure the financial story matches the business story. If the firm is said to be flying, but the numbers tell a different story, that's when you need to start asking more serious questions.

The bigger picture

While I am trawling through the numbers, I always have one eye on related systems and processes. I'm looking for how well the business runs without constant micromanagement. Are there clear systems and processes in place? Could a new hire follow their structure and get results, or is everything in someone's head?

Real due diligence goes deeper than just ticking boxes, making sure the accounts are in order and checking there is no dodgy legal stuff in the background. It's about getting a full picture, not just of the business itself, but the people, the culture, the customer journey and the market it operates in. I want to know if the company is overly reliant on one big client or one key supplier, because that's a risk. If one customer pulls out and the whole thing collapses, that's not a business, it's a ticking time bomb.

Leadership

One of the most important elements of the bigger picture is leadership. I've already talked about how

INVESTING IN OTHER BUSINESSES

to assess founders for a good fit, but you also need to look at who is running a business on a day-to-day basis – if they are not one and the same. This goes beyond the founder or CEO, to the full leadership team. I'll usually ask to speak with them directly, one on one if possible, to get a feel for who they are, how they think and what their roles are in the business.

I'll caveat this by saying, these meetings are not always possible, for example if the owner does not wish it to be known that they are exploring a sale. But if I do get access, I want to know who's actually involved in the day-to-day and who's just got a fancy job title.

In these meetings, I ask questions to find out:

- What they do
- What their background is
- What they think about the company's future
- Whether they are fully committed or just coasting
- How they feel about the business potentially being sold, scaled or changing direction

You'd be surprised how many people in senior roles are quite resistant to change, even if it's positive. Being too emotionally attached to doing things their way means they won't be able to adapt and will eventually hit a wall. I want to work with people who are sharp but still open to listening to other viewpoints.

Beyond the CV and the talk, I'm also looking at the dynamic between the team to see how they work together and if there is a culture of accountability and ownership. There is nothing more worrying than seeing everyone blaming each other for issues. If the leadership team isn't aligned, or if it's clear there's tension or politics going on, that's another red flag. A business can't grow with a dysfunctional top team, no matter how good the product is.

I also try to get a sense of how much of the business relies on one or two key people. If the founder disappears tomorrow, would the others step up and hold things together, or will it all fall apart? That kind of stability – or lack thereof – says a lot about whether the company can scale, sell or even survive long term. The business needs legs of its own.

Evaluating the leadership team means looking at mindset, chemistry, commitment and how they respond under pressure. A little humility is good, too. Leaders should be willing to admit what they don't know, because no one has all the answers.

Customers

Finally, the customer side is also important. Check how a business attracts and retains customers. This means exploring their churn rate to see if people are buying once and never coming back, or if there's real loyalty there. I'll also investigate online reviews, any feedback systems they use and even buy the product

INVESTING IN OTHER BUSINESSES

or service myself to experience it from a customer's point of view.

Proper due diligence isn't about looking for reasons to say yes. It's digging in deep to find any reasons to say no. If you skip this process or rush through it, you're basically gambling. Don't let yourself learn the hard way that a deal that looks shiny on the surface can cost you a fortune if you don't do the right digging.

> **Hustle mindset tips for spotting red flags**
>
> Over time, I've learned to spot quite a few red flags of a bad investment. If you see any of these, walk away:
>
> - **The founder is cagey or vague with information:** This is especially worrying if you ask for proper financials and they start dancing around the numbers, or give you bits and pieces instead of the full picture. Transparency is everything. If they're hiding stuff now, what else are they going to hide once you're involved?
>
> - **The business is completely dependent on the founder:** If they go on holiday for two weeks and everything falls apart, that's not a real business. That's just a person with a bunch of responsibilities and no structure behind them. You need to know the operation can stand on its own.
>
> - **Inflated egos:** When the top team acts like they've got all the answers, or they won't take feedback, that's a warning sign. I don't care how smart or successful someone is, if they can't

> admit they don't know something, or they think they're too big to fail, that arrogance usually catches up with them.
>
> - **Overpromising:** If someone's pitching an investment but everything's best-case scenario and they've not factored in any real-world risk, don't invest. You need realism, not fantasy. Be optimistic, sure, but back it up with facts.

My final piece of advice on investments is not to rush into anything. You've got to give it proper time and consideration. If I don't fully understand the business, the numbers, the people behind it and how it operates, then I'm not putting a penny in.

I might spend a few weeks, even a couple of months, going back and forth, asking questions, checking the accounts, digging into the backend and speaking to the team. I'll always take the time to spot the holes because once you're in, you're in. If you've missed something because you couldn't be bothered to dig a bit deeper, it'll cost you far more time and money in the long run. You're far more likely to regret making a decision too quickly, than taking your time.

14
The Exit

It makes sense to put a chapter about selling your business at the end of this book. The exit is, after all, the culmination of your entrepreneurial journey. You've come up with an idea, built a solid business and, all being well, now someone wants to buy it. You'll finally get the reward for all that pressure and hard work. I did hesitate about positioning it here though, because in reality, you need to be thinking about an exit from day one.

For clarity, when I talk about exit, I'm mostly referring to a private sale. All the other options – IPOs, mergers and management buyouts – are possible, but they're rare unless you're building at a certain scale or in a very specific sector. For the majority of founders, the most realistic outcome is selling their business privately to a competitor, a larger company or someone looking to break into their industry. Yet for most, they lose out on potential buyers or higher valuations due to incomplete financial records and poor business documentation.

Thinking long-term

Why do you need to plan so far ahead, particularly when just surviving day to day is challenging enough for a start-up? Because exiting well is a discipline. You need to design the business so that when the time comes, it's not just profitable, but running like a dream – the perfect package, ready to hand over to an eager buyer.

When I think back to the gaps I was confronted with in my earlier exits, the things I had to explain away or the times I had to accept a lower valuation because I hadn't put the right protections in place, I realise these were avoidable costs. Today, whether the goal is to sell in three years or thirty, I build as if a buyer were looking over my shoulder from day one. It's a mindset that turns the exit strategy from an afterthought into a source of competitive advantage. Far too few businesses think this way and have an exit strategy in place.

I'm not recommending this approach because I think you should look to bail at the earliest opportunity. It's because knowing your end goal shapes how you build the business in the first place. Right from the start, you should be thinking about what your aim is

THE EXIT

here. Do you want to run a massive multibillion-pound company and carry all the pressure, responsibilities and long-term commitment that comes with it? Or are you building something solid with the intention of exiting for a life-changing figure, enough to buy back your time, secure your future and give you freedom to invest in other projects, businesses or property?

Your answers to these questions affect everything, from how you structure the company, to how you build the team, to what kind of investors you bring in, even what kind of tech stack or branding decisions you make. If you don't have an exit in mind, you're just drifting.

You do, of course, need to be realistic. Many owners look at their businesses as their retirement plan, imagining a big payday when they sell. In truth, though, not every business is destined to be sold, no matter how well it performs. Some models are simply unsellable in practical terms. I'd class Wet Paws Dartford as one of these. This was my dog swimming pool business, which operated from two pools on rented land. It did fine as a source of income, but what buyer would take it on knowing they couldn't secure the same premises? Moving it twenty miles away would mean abandoning its customer base and, therefore, most of its value. When a business is tethered to circumstances that can't be transferred, its sale value is next to nothing.

Again, it is helpful if you think about the business in these terms from the off. You have two choices when you set up: either design it from the outset to be saleable, or accept that it's an income stream and not a nest egg. Right now, only two of my businesses have been built with a clear exit strategy in mind: Pulsare Pay, the fintech company, and the one focused on the findom adult entertainment industry. I've researched their scale, I understand the markets and I know they can command a serious valuation in the future if I get everything right. Other ventures I'm involved in, like certain niche e-commerce brands, are far less likely to attract a buyer outside of their specific sector. They might be profitable, but they're not designed for easy transfer to a willing buyer. Having said that, I would still recommend setting up businesses like these as though they were going to be sold. Doing so forces you to build watertight systems, maintain clear financials and keep strict operational discipline, all of which are crucial even outside of a sale situation. It's a much better way to run a business and, who knows, opportunities can appear unexpectedly. If your house is in order, you can take advantage of them.

Investment exits

There's one more caveat, before I get into the detail. Since I spoke about the power of becoming an investor in the previous chapter, I should also add that the exit approaches of someone who starts a business from scratch and someone who is an investor are completely different. When you start a business, you're in full control and can plan your ideal exit from the outset. You set your targets, build with the long game in mind and decide how many years you're willing to put in before you want to cash out or move on. But when you're investing in someone else's business, you're not in the driver's seat. Even so, you should still be thinking about your exit early on – at the time of entry. Since you're not calling the shots, your exit is going to depend heavily on the terms of the agreement you make going in. Most of the time, there'll be clauses in place, things like right of first refusal, where the founder or the company gets the first option to buy your shares if you want to exit. Sometimes you can cash out quickly, other times you'll find yourself locked in for a longer period if you don't take enough care to negotiate and agree your exit rights up front. Before you part with any money, you should be clear about how, when and to whom you can sell your investment.

Always be exit-ready

Even if you have no intention of putting a 'for sale' sign on your business tomorrow, you should run it as if a buyer might walk through the door at any moment. That mindset forces you to keep the numbers tight, the operations clean and the brand protected. This is key to building a genuinely healthy, resilient and valuable company. If and when an opportunity does appear, you won't have the luxury of months to tidy up and get everything in good shape. The work you've put into making it sale-ready from the start could well be the difference between scrambling to salvage a deal and commanding the price you deserve.

The key areas you should focus on are, at the very least, systems and processes, clean accounts, invoicing and payments and legal and compliance.

Let's break down what you should be looking for in each of these areas.

Preparing a business for exit

Systems and processes	Everything should run without you. From onboarding to customer service to fulfilment. Document everything so it's clear, repeatable and scalable.
Clean accounts	Make sure your P&L, balance sheet, cash flow and all financial reports are accurate and up to date. No buyer wants to see messy books or unexplained gaps. Get a solid accountant if you don't already have one.
Invoicing and payments	Keep everything tidy: money in, money out, no unpaid VAT and no dodgy creditor issues. All invoices should be easy to trace. Use cloud accounting software like Xero or QuickBooks if you aren't already doing so. (See Chapter 9.)
Legal and compliance	All contracts, employee agreements, supplier terms, IP and trademarks should be legally sound and easy to hand over.

If you let things drift, it can take up to a year to get some of the elements listed here into place and it is difficult to sell a business without them. Take trademarks, as a case in point. Buyers want to see these in place because, if you don't own the brand, someone else can step in, secure the rights and force the business owner to buy them back or lose the ability to operate under their own name. I learned this first-hand when I sold Trusted Training 4U. While the deal still went through, missing trademarks and other oversights lowered the valuation and delayed the sale. It was a sobering moment. Now, I approach these details not as bureaucratic chores but as investments in the company's future worth. They're as critical to the exit as the product itself.

Get going on these things as soon as you can because it's a very slow process – the time spent securing trademarks for my findom and fintech businesses can be measured in years, not months. Since these are the two businesses I have earmarked for an eventual exit, the pressure was on. In both cases, the processes were anything but straightforward. There were challenges with the names we chose for the brands, which meant endless back and forth with lawyers to get it sorted. My advice: start now.

When's the right time to exit?

After all that prep, how do you know when the time is right to sell? It usually boils down to two forces: what's happening inside your business, and what's happening outside in the market. The trick is to keep a clear view of both.

External signs

Let's start with the outside. If the landscape around you is shifting, new technology is disrupting your sector, customer habits are changing and competitors are moving fast, but you're not interested in a pivot, that's a flashing light signalling that a change is needed. A good example would be if AI is creeping into your space and you're not planning for how to integrate it or evolve alongside it. In this case, the clock is ticking and this might be the moment to exit while your position is still strong, rather than waiting until you're playing catch-up and your business looks outdated. The question here isn't whether the business can survive, but whether you want to keep pace with where the world is going.

The opposite is also true. If your industry is on the brink of a boom, it rarely makes sense to walk away before the wave hits. That's the time to either dig in deeper, or ride it out until you can command a premium price. Even then, timing matters. Some entrepreneurs try to time the sale to just before the peak, knowing that the post-boom hangover can be brutal – increased competition, market saturation and tougher regulations can eat into value fast. It's tricky to get right though.

For some founders, the decision comes when an offer lands on the table from someone who sees hidden value in their sector. It's quite rare, but if the price is right and the deal terms work, it's worth considering. In this case, you'll need to weigh up what you'd walk away with against what you'd be leaving behind. Sometimes it's a reactive decision, but it can still be a strategic one. You've simply been given an opportunity that makes sense.

Internal signs

Inside the business, the warning signs that it could be time to exit can be more subtle. You may see growth starting to plateau, overheads creeping up, cash flow getting tight, or the team showing signs of burnout. If the energy is draining out of the business and it's not just a short-term dip, it's time to take a hard look at your options.

It could also be that your own passions have shifted. Maybe another venture is calling your attention, or you just don't have the drive to push this business forwards anymore. It's not always about underperformance; the business might be thriving, but you're no longer in step with it or as emotionally invested as you once were. You'll feel that before you consciously admit it, but when you notice it, it is often the sign that it's time to start thinking about moving on. In my experience, exits are often sparked by either strategic foresight or emotional readiness. The best results happen when you read the signs early and make a move while you still have momentum.

Ultimately, whether you're approached or you initiate the sale, the decision comes down to timing, mindset and vision. If an exit opens the door to something that excites you more than what you're doing today, that's usually all the clarity you need.

Maximising the sale price

A good exit is your reward for the years of work, sacrifice and risk. The money you walk away with isn't just a number in the bank; it's a validation of your vision and confirmation that what you built had real value in the market.

To me, a successful exit means two key things: timing it right and walking away with a solid profit. Too many founders get caught chasing bigger numbers or trying to hold onto control for too long, and they miss the moment. The sweet spot is when you recognise that you've built enough value, the market conditions are right and there's someone willing to pay what it's truly worth – or, even better, will overpay because they see future potential.

Maximising the sale price requires putting yourself in the buyer's shoes. They need to believe the business won't crumble the moment you leave, which is where all those fundamentals like good systems and clean accounts come into their own. Buyers are looking for stability and scalability, so recurring revenue streams, low customer churn, strong brand presence, intellectual property and a capable team will all push your valuation upwards. You also want to show the buyer that there is untapped growth potential; in other words, give them a clear roadmap of opportunities they can capitalise on. Do this, and the sale price will be based on what could happen in the future, rather than just what is going on now. The less risk they perceive, the more they'll pay. A business that's prepared for the future is worth more than one that's peaked.

Something you'll need to think very hard about is what would happen if you left. If your name, face or leadership is tied closely to the brand, you won't be exiting overnight. On the other hand, if your business can run without you, supported by recurring revenue, documented systems and clean financials, you're in a stronger position to command a higher multiple and negotiate better terms. The most valuable companies are those where the owner could disappear tomorrow and the business wouldn't skip a beat. That means there has to be a brilliant team in place that's motivated to stay on after the handover.

Ideally, there will be more than one buyer in the mix. If so, you'll gain leverage that you can use to strike a deal that aligns with your vision, whether that's maximum cash at completion or an ongoing stake in future growth.

Ultimately, it's about positioning. You're not just selling a business, you're selling an opportunity and the more you can de-risk that opportunity for the buyer, the more they'll be willing to pay.

The key financial metrics

Buyers typically focus on a handful of key financial metrics to assess the value, health and potential of a business. These metrics not only help them evaluate the risk and return, but also influence the final valuation multiple they're willing to pay.

Key financial metrics for a sale

Revenue/ turnover	Buyers look at total revenue trends over the past two to three years. Ideally, these should show consistent growth.
EBITDA (Earnings Before Interest, Taxes, Depreciation and Amortisation)	This is one of the most used metrics when valuing a company. In the UK, SMEs typically sell at a multiple of 2–5x EBITDA, depending on sector, risk and scale.
Gross profit margin	Strong margins signal operational efficiency and pricing power. Most buyers will want to see at least 30–40% margins for product-based businesses and 50–70%+ for service-based ones.
Net profit/net margin	Buyers assess profitability after all expenses to gauge sustainability. A business consistently netting upwards of 10–20% margin is generally attractive to buyers.
Cash flow	Consistent positive cash flow shows the business can sustain itself without external funding. Buyers may review free cash flow to understand how much cash is available after capital expenditure and other obligations.
Customer concentration	If a large percentage of revenue comes from just one or two clients, that's a risk. Ideally, no single client should represent more than 10–15% of total turnover.
Recurring revenue	Subscription models, retainers and long-term contracts increase value.

Managing the sale

Managing the sale of a business is a project in its own right and the more smoothly that process runs, the better your chances of securing the price, terms and timing you want. There are a few things to consider here.

Professional advice

Most founders only sell a business once in their lifetime, twice at a push, but professional advisers do it all the time. This is why bringing in the professionals can make all the difference between a clean, profitable exit and a deal that drags or falls apart entirely.

At the *very least* you need a strong legal team who will guide you through contracts, due diligence, share purchase agreements and NDAs, making sure you don't give away intellectual property, accept unfair warranties or agree to take on liabilities that come back to haunt you. Legal delays are one of the top reasons deals collapse, so having a solicitor experienced in business sales is critical. Alongside them, your accountant plays a dual role, presenting your numbers in the most buyer-friendly way and ensuring the structure of the sale and the transaction itself are as tax-efficient as possible.

Another option to consider is bringing in consultants, exit advisers and brokers to act as the architects of the process. These experts will help prepare and position your business for sale, identify the right buyers, manage confidentiality and negotiate terms. A good broker will create competitive tension between buyers, giving you leverage on both price and conditions. Most will charge a success fee, anywhere from 3% to 10%, but in many cases, their input pays for itself in the uplift they achieve on the final deal.

Transparency

Preparation for a sale is about more than simply managing paperwork and bringing good advisers. A successful sale is also predicated on effectively managing your team. Early in the process, it's wise to keep discussions about what is going on limited to trusted senior team members who will be directly involved in preparing the business for sale. They need context, clarity and reassurance about what's coming, because their cooperation is often part of the value that you're selling. For the rest of the team, timing is everything. I would strongly advise waiting until the deal is far enough along to be more likely than not to complete. Sharing too early risks distracting the team from the day job and causing unnecessary anxiety – and you don't want your best people to start polishing their CVs.

The same principle applies to customers. If the sale will directly affect them – through changes in ownership, branding or service – it needs to be communicated at the right time, in a clear and positive way. They don't need the full backstory, but they do need to feel confident that their experience of your business will either remain stable or improve. The goal is to maintain trust and minimise disruption while the transaction is underway.

Managing your own exit

Finally, expect negotiation around your role after the sale. Some buyers will want a full handover, keeping you on for six to twelve months, or even longer, while others may want a quick, clean break with you out of the door.

Achieving a smooth process is about managing every moving part, legal, financial, operational and human, so that the transition is seamless for all involved and the value you've built transfers cleanly and in its entirety to the next owner.

Misconceptions about selling

It might need to go without saying, but sometimes you do need to state the obvious: a business is never sold until it is sold. Things can easily stall, or collapse, and there are a few common misconceptions and mistakes that make these outcomes more likely.

When I tried to sell the training company because it was all getting too much, I made a bunch of mistakes. My first big error was deciding to sell out of neglect rather than from a position of strength. My attention had been consumed by the restaurant and other projects, and the business had already been drifting for a while. The numbers had slipped, systems had become untidy and it had lost the shine that buyers like to see. Had I maintained its performance from a year or so earlier, I could have secured three to five times the price I eventually accepted.

As well as a lower sale price, the business spent six to eight months on the market before it sold. In that time, my disengagement made the decline worse, compounding the initial mistake I'd made on timing. Every month, revenue weakened. When you're selling, buyers want to see your most recent bank statements and accounts and, in my case, the picture at the start of the sale process was very different from the one at the end. I had initially listed the business for £253,000, a price I was told was realistic, but by the time we closed the deal, I accepted £170,000, almost half the original target. The drop was entirely down to the fact I'd taken my foot off the gas.

At one stage, I had genuine interest from a buyer who was ready to move forward. Then they went quiet for months, only to return asking for updated accounts. By then, the decline was plain to see and they came back with a lower offer. I couldn't really argue or negotiate my way out of it because the numbers told the true story. It was a sobering lesson in how the momentum of a business is as much of an asset as its tangible infrastructure.

If I had simply held things steady, maintained sales, kept the books tight and presented a business that was consistently in full working order, I could have doubled my return. Instead, I let day-to-day distractions undermine the deal. Since then, I have taken the opposite approach. From day one, I build all of my businesses as if the buyer is already in the room, making sure they are ready to command top value when the time comes. Importantly, that process continues even after the sale process has begun.

> **Hustle mindset tips for staying grounded when selling a business**
>
> - **Be patient:** A lot of founders underestimate how complex and drawn-out the sale process can be. It's not a simple list-it-and-sell-it affair. If you're serious about an exit, you've got to be realistic. It could take between six months and a year, more if it is complex.
> - **Not all buyer interest is genuine:** You do get a lot of tyre kickers in this game. Some only want to see documentation to get a better handle on the industry, perhaps because they're already in discussion to buy a rival firm. It is crucial to qualify buyers upfront for motivation, industry knowledge and financial capability.
> - **Look beyond the highest bid:** While tempting to go with the biggest offer, it may not always be the best. Terms matter just as much, if not more, than 'the number'. A lower offer with secure financing and clean terms often beats a high bid that may collapse in due diligence. Some buyers insist on complex earn-outs or heavy contingencies that reduce the real value of their bid.

No deal

Bear in mind that if the sale collapses altogether, or if no willing buyer can be found, you will need to think about a Plan B. Sometimes, a business just doesn't work, plain and simple. You've got to know when to call it. You can't let ego or sunk cost drag you down with it. It's easy to keep pouring in more money, time and energy, thinking you're one move away from turning it around. But if a business is done, all you're doing is prolonging the inevitable and burning yourself out in the process.

There comes a point where you've got to take a step back and ask: *Is this still serving me?* I don't mean just financially, but mentally and emotionally too. If the answer's no, then walking away might be the strongest move you can make. It's not failure; it's a pivot. Sometimes it is better to have the clarity and foresight to cut your losses, take the lessons and redirect that energy into something better.

Most start-ups fail. That's the reality. The difference between those who bounce back and those who burn out is knowing when to stop. I've walked away from projects that had potential, but the timing was wrong, the team was off or the market wasn't there. There's never any shame in that. Treat it like an investment. If it's not performing, you divest. Then you regroup, recalibrate and go again, with sharper instincts and thicker skin.

Life after the sale

Life after selling a business isn't always the champagne-popping, problem-free chapter that one might imagine. In reality, it can be more complex than building the company in the first place. The sale might bring a surge of cash, which is always welcome, but also arrives with a wave of decisions. You now need to think about how to handle tax liabilities, invest and protect the proceeds and navigate any new regulatory obligations. Perhaps most surprisingly of all, you'll also need to think about how to fill the gap in your identity and daily structure once the business is gone. I've known a lot of sellers who find themselves restless or unfulfilled, missing the sense of purpose they had while running their venture.

The entrepreneurs who handle this transition best are those who can separate their identity from their business. It's natural to feel emotionally tied to something you've built, but over-identifying can cloud judgement and make it harder to let go. Founders who find a way to keep a clear boundary between themselves and their business will experience less stress, recover faster from setbacks and are more likely to enjoy engaging with new ventures. By seeing the business as a separate entity, with its own life cycle, you can exit with more clarity, less turmoil and greater readiness for what's next.

The way to see an exit is as both an ending and a beginning. For the entrepreneurially minded, a sale is rarely about 'cashing out and walking away' forever. It's a pivot point. Sometimes that pivot comes from strength, other times from necessity. The 'what next' is crucial, though. The smoothest transitions happen when you have a post-sale plan, whether that's starting a new venture, joining another company, investing in other businesses or even taking a break. For me, what's made it easier is not walking away into nothing. Just like you might not leave a job without lining up another one, I wouldn't shut down or sell a business unless I've already got something else in motion, whether that's a new venture or even just a clear idea of where I'm heading next. Having that next direction in mind gives you focus, momentum and a sense of control, and avoids that feeling of loss. Without a focus for your energy, it's easy to drift or dwell on what you've left behind.

Selling your business is not the final chapter of your entrepreneurial story, it's just the end of that particular book. The knowledge, skills and networks you've built stay with you even after a sale or closure. If you're wired like a true entrepreneur, you'll already be thinking about the next idea, the next market and next challenge. This is just the clearing of the slate, making room for whatever comes next.

Conclusion

For me, success has never been about Lambos or flashy watches. It's about freedom. Financial freedom, yes, but also the freedom of not having to answer to anyone, being able to make my own decisions and, most importantly, being in control of my own time and my own life. Success is waking up each day and knowing you're building something that's yours. It's about progress, because if you're not moving forward, what are you doing?

The idea of doing anything else scares me. Too many people become slaves to the system, making it seem normal. You spend the best years of your life waking up to an alarm, sitting in traffic or crammed on public transport, working all day to make someone else rich, coming home exhausted and repeating it all over again. Eat, sleep, work, repeat. That's what they want for you. That's what's been designed for you.

And the worst part? People accept it. They don't question it. They don't even realise they're trapped.

I've seen it happen time and time again. For some people, when they get locked into this system, they stop progressing and lose purpose. They stop looking after themselves, mentally and physically. They become depressed, demotivated and disconnected. A lot of that stems from the loss of momentum and the absence of a goal or vision to move toward. The daily grind is not for people with a hustle mindset.

You don't have to accept the life that's been handed to you, if you don't want it. You can build your own, on your own terms. Right now, you have a choice. You can close this book, carry on as you were and stay in the same cycle, or you can do something about it. You can take action, start small, make mistakes and keep moving forward until you've built something that belongs to you.

No one is coming to save you. The system is designed to keep you locked in. The only way out is to hustle. You can escape the system by running your own business. Not just for the money, although that's a part of it, but for the ability to own your time, make your own decisions and take control of your future.

Over the course of this book, I've shared some of the most important lessons I've learned, in order to help you on your way. I've explained how:

- **Ideas are worthless without execution.**
  Everyone has ideas, but only a handful of people act on them. Be in that handful.

- **Your first business will teach you more than any course ever could.** Don't wait for the perfect moment though, it doesn't exist. Start now, make mistakes and learn fast.

- **The business landscape is ever evolving.** What works today might be obsolete tomorrow. Stay informed about industry trends, be open to feedback and don't be afraid to pivot your strategy when necessary. Adaptability can be the difference between growth and stagnation.

- **Partnerships can make or break you.** Choose your business partners wisely, have the tough conversations early and make sure everything is watertight from day one.

- **Build a team that believes in you.** When money is tight, vision is everything. If people believe in where you're going, they'll stick with you through the tough times.

- **Treat your team like a family.** You rely on them and they rely on you. Build a culture of trust, loyalty and shared ambition.

- **Prioritise systems and processes.** Every business has shit to deal with. If you don't sort these out early, you'll be drowning in chaos before you even get started.

- **Your time is your most valuable asset.** Diversify carefully, focus on what actually makes a difference and don't spread yourself too thin.

- **Look after your mental state.** You can have all the money in the world, but if you're mentally caged, it means nothing. Break away from the system, cut out the people holding you back and take control of your life.
- **Don't be greedy.** Invest in businesses and collaborate with the best. A piece of something great is better than all of something small. The right partnerships will take you further, faster and give you the freedom to do more of what you truly enjoy.

I truly hope that this book hasn't scared you off from starting your own business. That was never the goal. I didn't write *The Hustle Mindset* to sell you a dream of overnight success, or to tell you a feel-good story about how easy it is to make it as an entrepreneur. I wrote it to tell you the truth, the real truth, about what it takes to build something from nothing. If you're serious about creating a life on your own terms, you need to know exactly what you're up against.

If you are feeling a little unsure right now – I get it. Uncertainty is part of the game. Remember what separates the hustlers from the dreamers, though. If you can't stomach it, you shouldn't be in business, because there will be days where everything feels like it's hanging by a thread. Cash flow gets tight, staff issues pile up, deals fall through and you start questioning whether the whole thing could collapse tomorrow. That feeling is real and it happens again and again. What matters is how you handle it.

CONCLUSION

If something scares me, I take that as a sign that I need to do it. Every time I've done something I feared, whether it was launching a new business, taking a risk on someone, speaking in front of an audience or backing myself with money I couldn't afford to lose, I've grown. Fear is a signal. It shows you where the growth is. You won't grow if you keep doing the same things and talking to the same people. That's how to get left behind.

Staying in your comfort zone is dangerous. If you're not uncomfortable, you're not growing. Sure, it's easy to stick to what you know, to just rinse and repeat what's worked before, but where's the fun in that? Who wants to stay in a mindless system, just about staying afloat until retirement? Start a business, grow and evolve. Embrace the idea of trying new strategies, testing new platforms, investing in new tech and constantly adapting to what's coming next. The people who grow are the ones who move with the world, not the ones who let it pass them by.

Not everything you try will work. As you've seen, I've had my fair share of failures, setbacks and, let's face it, absolute disasters. I've lost money, made the wrong calls and trusted the wrong people. But I kept going, and that's why I'm still here and have managed to build businesses that have given me the freedom to live life on my own terms.

I live by everything I have talked about in this book and still feel like I am learning every single day. The hustle mindset drives me to constantly educate myself. If I don't understand something, I'll go and learn it,

THE HUSTLE MINDSET

whether it's AI, payment tech, automation, marketing or just how to manage people better. I always throw myself into it. It might feel uncomfortable at first learning something new, but once I get a grip on it, I'm ahead of the game. That edge increases over time.

The hustle mindset never ends, but neither should your growth. This mindset will change everything.

So, what are you going to do next?

Acknowledgements

Thanks go out to my business partners, in particular Poppy, Nick and Alex, who all deserve recognition for what they do. It has been a pleasure to work alongside them as we build businesses together and find answers to problems big and small. A big shout-out goes to the team, too – those who have worked on my businesses, large and small, successful and unsuccessful. Despite the challenges we've faced, you've always been there and it has not gone unnoticed. You've all got the hustle mindset.

I'd also like to thank every individual who has been there for some part of this journey, even when it hasn't gone well. It's only by seeing how things shouldn't be done that you learn how to do them better.

THE HUSTLE MINDSET

Last but not least, I'd like to say a big thank you to everyone who helped me get this book out into the market. It's been on my to-do list for a while, and it's great to finally have it out there.

The Author

Reece Borg is an entrepreneur based in London. He has founded, scaled and exited multiple businesses across finance, e-commerce, fitness and technology. He is the founder of RB Business Consultancy, where he works selectively with founders and owners/operators at key decision points, helping them navigate growth, risk and uncertainty. His work focuses less on theory and more on judgement, pattern recognition and long-term thinking.

🌐 www.rbbusinessconsultancy.co.uk

www.ingramcontent.com/pod-product-compliance
Lightning Source LLC
Chambersburg PA
CBHW011404210526
45464CB00010B/3037